GOODSON MUMBA

Unveiling Zambia's Potential

Opportunities for Profitable Investment

Copyright © 2024 by Goodson Mumba

All rights reserved. No part of this publication may be reproduced, stored or transmitted in any form or by any means, electronic, mechanical, photocopying, recording, scanning, or otherwise without written permission from the publisher. It is illegal to copy this book, post it to a website, or distribute it by any other means without permission.

First edition

ISBN: 9798336055054

This book was professionally typeset on Reedsy. Find out more at reedsy.com

Contents

Preface iv
Acknowledgments vii
Dedication viii
Disclaimer ix
1 Chapter 1: Introduction to Zambia 1
2 Chapter 2: Zambia's Booming Sectors 19
3 Chapter 3: Infrastructure Developments in Zambia 39
4 Chapter 4: Government Incentives for Investors 59
5 Chapter 5: Setting Up a Business in Zambia 80
6 Chapter 6: Labor Market and Human Resources 100
7 Chapter 7: Land Acquisition and Property Rights 113
8 Chapter 8: Sustainable Business Practices in Zambia 127
9 Chapter 9: Market Research and Due Diligence 137
10 Chapter 10: The Future of Investment in Zambia 144
About the Author 152

Preface

Zambia, a land of breathtaking landscapes, rich cultural heritage, and abundant natural resources, stands on the brink of a new era of economic prosperity. As the world increasingly looks towards emerging markets for investment opportunities, Zambia presents a unique proposition with its stable political climate, forward-thinking economic policies, and strategic position within Southern Africa. This book, "Unveiling Zambia's Potential: Opportunities for Profitable Investment," seeks to illuminate the vast opportunities that lie within this dynamic and vibrant nation.

The journey of compiling this comprehensive guide has been driven by a deep-seated belief in Zambia's potential and the desire to share this vision with investors, policymakers, and entrepreneurs around the globe. As the authors, we have drawn upon our extensive experience in the fields of economics, business development, and international trade to provide a detailed and nuanced understanding of the investment landscape in Zambia.

This book is structured to offer readers a clear and thorough roadmap for navigating the myriad opportunities and challenges associated with investing in Zambia. From the rich agricultural lands that promise high yields and profitability, to the untapped mineral resources that are critical in the global shift towards green energy, each chapter is designed to provide actionable insights and practical guidance.

In "Unveiling Zambia's Potential," you will find an in-depth analysis of key sectors such as agriculture, mining, manufacturing, tourism, and financial services. We explore the latest developments in infrastructure, energy, and telecommunications, highlighting how these advancements are transforming Zambia into an investment haven. The book also delves into the intricacies of setting up a business, the legal and regulatory framework, and the various incentives offered by the government to attract and protect investors.

Understanding the context of Zambia's economic evolution is crucial for any prospective investor. Therefore, we provide a historical overview of investment in Zambia, examining the colonial and post-colonial economic trajectories and the significant reforms that have shaped the current business environment. Additionally, we offer projections for the future, identifying emerging trends and sectors with high growth potential.

The insights contained within these pages are not merely theoretical. They are supported by case studies, interviews with key stakeholders, and firsthand experiences that offer a realistic perspective on what it means to invest in Zambia. We aim to equip you with the knowledge and tools necessary to make informed investment decisions that are both profitable and sustainable.

As Zambia continues to make strides towards achieving its Vision 2030 goals, we invite you to join us in this exciting journey of growth and transformation. "Unveiling Zambia's Potential" is more than just a book; it is a call to action for those who see beyond the present and are willing to invest in the future of one of Africa's most promising economies.

We hope that this book inspires you to explore the vast opportunities that Zambia has to offer and that it serves as a valuable resource in your investment endeavors. Together, let us unveil Zambia's potential and contribute to its story of progress and prosperity.

Sincerely,

Goodson Mumba

Acknowledgments

I would like to eternally and gratefully acknowledge the Almighty God for the infinite intelligence from His universal mind where we draw from all that we come to know and are yet to know. May I also acknowledge and thank everyone that has played a part in my journey of life in terms of spiritual, moral, emotional and material support.

Dedication

I extend my sincerest gratitude to my beloved wife, Edith Mumba, and our children, Angelina, Lubuto, Letticia, Lulumbi, and Butusho, for their unwavering support and understanding throughout the conception, writing, and eventual publication of this book, despite the sacrifices and challenges they endured.

Disclaimer

This book is a work of fiction. Names, characters, businesses, places, events, and incidents are either the products of the author's imagination or used in a fictitious manner. Any resemblance to actual persons, living or dead, or actual events is purely coincidental.

1

Chapter 1: Introduction to Zambia

Geography and Demographics

The bustling conference hall in Lusaka was filled with energy as entrepreneurs, investors, and experts gathered for the summit. At the center of it all was Chanda Mwamba, who had worked tirelessly to organize this event. As the attendees settled into their seats, Chanda took to the stage, ready to kick off the summit with a deep dive into Zambia's geography and demographics.

Chanda began with a broad smile, "Welcome everyone to the heart of Zambia! Today, we start our journey by understanding the very land we stand on and the people who call it home."

He clicked the remote, and a large map of Zambia appeared on the screen behind him.

Location and Physical Landscape

"Zambia is a landlocked country in the heart of Southern Africa," Chanda explained. "We share borders with eight countries: Tanzania to the northeast, Malawi to the east, Mozambique to the southeast, Zimbabwe and Botswana to the south, Namibia to the southwest, Angola to the west, and the Democratic Republic of the Congo to the north."

Kalenga Mukuka, a respected mining engineer, nodded in agreement. "The diversity of our landscape is impressive. From the mineral-rich regions of the Copperbelt to the vast plains of the Kafue National Park, Zambia is a treasure trove of natural beauty and resources."

Chanda continued, "We have three major rivers – the Zambezi, Kafue, and Luangwa – which not only support our agriculture but also attract tourists from around the world. The Victoria Falls, one of the Seven Natural Wonders, is a testament to our country's breathtaking landscapes."

Population Distribution and Urbanization

Mutinta Mwiinga raised her hand to add, "Our population is approximately 18 million, and it's growing rapidly. About 40% of our people live in urban areas, with Lusaka and the Copperbelt being the most densely populated regions. This urbanization trend offers both opportunities and challenges for infrastructure development and service delivery."

Wamundila Chikumbi, the influential lawyer, chimed in, "Indeed, the urban-rural divide is significant. While our cities are expanding, we must ensure that rural areas are not left behind. Investment in rural development is crucial for balanced growth."

Ethnic Groups and Cultural Diversity

Chanda smiled as he moved to the next topic. "One of the most enriching aspects of Zambia is our cultural diversity. We are home to over 70 ethnic groups, each with its own unique traditions and languages. This diversity is our strength and an integral part of our national identity."

Thandiwe Zulu, the financial expert, added passionately, "Our cultural festivals, such as the Kuomboka of the Lozi people and the Nc'wala of the Ngoni, are not just celebrations but also opportunities for cultural tourism and economic activity. Embracing our diversity can lead to inclusive growth."

Mutinta nodded, "Absolutely. Each ethnic group brings something unique to the table. From the traditional crafts of the Eastern Province to the vibrant music and dance of the Western Province, our cultural heritage is a valuable asset."

Chanda concluded, "Understanding our geography and demographics is the first step in unveiling Zambia's potential. Our land and our people are the foundation upon which we can build a prosperous future. Let's use this knowledge to inform our investment strategies and ensure that growth benefits all Zambians."

As the session ended, the attendees buzzed with excitement and curiosity, eager to explore the next chapters of Zambia's potential. The summit had just begun, but the vision for a brighter future was already taking shape.

Political and Economic Climate

The second day of the summit dawned bright and clear, with anticipation in the air. As participants filled the hall, Chanda Mwamba was already at the podium, ready to delve into Zambia's political and economic climate. He knew that understanding the governance and economic frameworks was crucial for potential investors.

Chanda began, "Good morning, everyone. Today, we shift our focus to the political and economic landscape of Zambia, exploring how governance, policies, and our role in international organizations shape our investment environment."

Governance and Political Stability

Wamundila Chikumbi, known for his legal acumen, stood up first. "Let's talk about governance. Zambia has enjoyed relative political stability since gaining independence in 1964. Our multiparty democratic system, despite its challenges, has seen peaceful transitions of power."

Chanda nodded, adding, "Stability is a key factor for investors. Our judiciary is independent, and there's a robust framework for protecting property rights and enforcing contracts. This stability provides a secure environment for business operations."

Kalenga Mukuka interjected, "While we are politically stable, we must continuously work on improving governance. Transparent institutions and the fight against corruption are ongoing battles. But overall, our political climate has been conducive to business growth."

Economic Policies and Reforms

Mutinta Mwiinga took the floor, "On the economic front, Zambia has implemented significant reforms over the years. The liberalization of our economy in the 1990s paved the way for private sector growth. We've seen reforms in the agricultural sector, aimed at boosting productivity and encouraging investment."

Thandiwe Zulu, with her expertise in finance, elaborated, "Our economic policies have focused on diversification, moving away from reliance on copper to include agriculture, tourism, and manufacturing. The introduction of the National Development Plans has provided a strategic framework for sustainable economic growth."

Chanda highlighted, "Recently, the government has introduced measures to improve the business environment. These include tax incentives for new investments, simplification of business registration processes, and improvements in infrastructure. These reforms are designed to make Zambia an attractive destination for investors."

Wamundila added, "However, economic policies must be dynamic and responsive to global trends. For instance, our recent engagement with the International Monetary Fund (IMF) aims to address fiscal challenges and ensure macroeconomic stability. Such steps are crucial for maintaining investor confidence."

Role in Regional and International Organizations

Mukuka Kapijimpanga then spoke, "Zambia's role in regional and international organizations also enhances our investment appeal. As a member of the Southern African Development Community (SADC) and the Common Market for Eastern and Southern Africa (COMESA), we have access to larger markets and regional trade opportunities."

Chanda expanded, "Our participation in these organizations fosters regional integration, which is vital for trade and investment. Moreover, Zambia's adherence to international standards and practices is seen in our involvement with the African Union (AU) and the United Nations (UN). These affiliations not only open doors for international cooperation but also reassure investors of our commitment to global norms."

Thandiwe added, "Additionally, our strategic position as a land-linked country makes us a key player in regional logistics and trade. Initiatives like the African Continental Free Trade Area (AfCFTA) present immense opportunities for cross-border investments and trade."

Chanda concluded, "In summary, Zambia's political stability, progressive economic policies, and active role in regional and international organizations create a promising environment for investment. By understanding these dynamics, we can better navigate the opportunities and challenges that lie ahead."

As the session wrapped up, participants buzzed with discussions, reflecting on the insights shared. The political and economic landscape of Zambia, as painted by the speakers, provided a solid foundation for the investment explorations that would follow in the summit.

Historical Overview of Investment in Zambia

The third day of the summit began with a palpable sense of excitement as attendees filled the conference hall. Chanda Mwamba, ready to guide them through Zambia's historical investment landscape, stood at the podium. The presentation aimed to provide context on how past investments had shaped the current economic climate and what lessons could be learned for future endeavors.

Chanda greeted everyone, "Good morning, and welcome to our third session. Today, we'll dive into the historical overview of investment in Zambia, tracing the journey from colonial times to the present day."

Colonial and Post-colonial Economic History

Wamundila Chikumbi, the lawyer with a keen interest in history, stood to speak first. "Let's start with the colonial era. During British colonial rule, Zambia, then Northern Rhodesia, was primarily exploited for its mineral wealth, especially copper. The British South Africa Company controlled large tracts of land and mineral rights, leading to significant but highly extractive investments."

Mutinta Mwiinga added, "Agriculture was also influenced by colonial policies, focusing on cash crops like maize and tobacco, often at the expense of subsistence farming. This period laid the foundation for Zambia's reliance on copper and monoculture agriculture."

Chanda continued, "After gaining independence in 1964, Zambia embarked on a path of nationalization under President Kenneth Kaunda. Key industries, including mining, were nationalized in the early 1970s, aiming to ensure that the benefits of these resources were distributed among Zambians."

Kalenga Mukuka, the mining engineer, interjected, "While nationalization initially boosted employment and social services, it eventually led to inefficiencies and declining production. By the late 1980s, the global drop in copper prices severely impacted the economy, highlighting the risks of over-reliance on a single commodity."

Major Historical Investments and Their Impact

Thandiwe Zulu took the stage, "Moving into the post-colonial period, one of the major historical investments was the establishment of the Kariba Dam in the 1950s, a joint venture with Zimbabwe. This massive hydroelectric project was crucial for energy supply but also had significant social and environmental impacts."

Chanda nodded, "Another landmark investment was the TAZARA Railway, completed in 1975 with Chinese assistance. This railway connected Zambia to the Tanzanian port of Dar es Salaam, crucial for landlocked Zambia's trade and export routes."

Mutinta pointed out, "The post-privatization era of the 1990s saw major investments from multinational companies in the mining sector. Companies like Vedanta and Glencore invested heavily in copper mines, modernizing operations and boosting production. However, these investments also brought challenges, including debates over labor conditions and environmental practices."

Evolution of Foreign Direct Investment (FDI)

Mukuka Kapijimpanga then spoke, "The liberalization of the economy in the 1990s marked a turning point. The government implemented policies to attract foreign direct investment (FDI), including tax incentives and legal reforms. This era saw a diversification of investment beyond mining, into sectors like agriculture, tourism, and manufacturing."

Thandiwe added, "FDI inflows increased significantly during the 2000s, driven by stable macroeconomic policies and political stability. Key sectors like telecommunications saw substantial investments, leading to the rapid expansion of mobile networks and internet services."

Chanda elaborated, "Today, FDI continues to play a vital role in Zambia's economic development. The establishment of Special Economic Zones and investment promotion agencies like the Zambia Development Agency (ZDA) are efforts to attract and retain foreign investors. These initiatives aim to create a more conducive environment for both domestic and foreign investments."

Kalenga concluded, "The evolution of FDI in Zambia has shown that while external investments are crucial for growth, it's equally important to ensure that these investments are sustainable and beneficial to the local population. Learning from our history, we can build a more resilient and inclusive economy."

Chanda smiled, "Indeed. Understanding our past investments helps us appreciate the complexities and opportunities in our current landscape. As we move forward, let's leverage these lessons to create a brighter future for Zambia."

The session ended with thoughtful discussions and reflections. The historical context provided a rich backdrop for the ongoing exploration of Zambia's investment potential, setting the stage for the practical sessions that would follow.

Zambia's Economic Indicators

On the fourth day of the summit, the attendees were abuzz with anticipation. Today's session promised to delve into the critical economic indicators that underpin Zambia's economic health and investment potential. Chanda Mwamba, ever the enthusiastic host, stood ready at the podium.

"Good morning, everyone," Chanda began. "Today, we will examine Zambia's economic indicators, which provide a snapshot of our economic health and inform our investment decisions. Let's start with GDP growth rates, inflation, and exchange rates, and finally, trade balance and key export-import data."

GDP Growth Rates

Thandiwe Zulu, the financial expert, stepped forward. "Let's look at GDP growth rates. Zambia has experienced variable GDP growth over the past decades. In the early 2000s, we saw robust growth averaging around 6-7% annually, primarily driven by the mining sector."

Chanda added, "This period of growth was a result of rising copper prices and significant foreign direct investments in mining. However, our growth rates have faced challenges due to fluctuations in global commodity prices and domestic economic policies."

Mutinta Mwiinga spoke up, "In recent years, diversification

efforts have aimed to stabilize growth. Agriculture, manufacturing, and services sectors have shown potential, though the transition has been gradual. The COVID-19 pandemic also impacted our growth, with the economy contracting in 2020."

Kalenga Mukuka nodded, "Yes, but recent data indicates a recovery phase with projections of 3-4% growth as the global economy stabilizes and domestic policies support business activities."

Inflation and Exchange Rates

Chanda continued, "Now, let's discuss inflation and exchange rates. Thandiwe, could you provide some insights?"

Thandiwe replied, "Certainly. Zambia has historically struggled with high inflation, particularly in the late 1980s and early 1990s, reaching hyperinflation levels. However, macroeconomic reforms and prudent fiscal policies in the 2000s helped bring inflation down to single digits for several years."

Mutinta added, "Despite these improvements, inflation spiked again in recent years due to factors like currency depreciation, rising food prices, and external economic shocks. The kwacha, our local currency, has also been volatile, impacting import costs and overall economic stability."

Chanda pointed out, "In response, the Bank of Zambia has implemented monetary policies to stabilize inflation and the exchange rate. Efforts to build foreign reserves and manage fiscal deficits are ongoing to support a stable economic environment."

Trade Balance and Key Export-Import Data

Wamundila Chikumbi took the floor, "Trade balance is a crucial indicator of economic health. Zambia's trade has been traditionally dominated by copper exports, which account for over 70% of our export earnings. This dependence makes our trade balance highly sensitive to global copper prices."

Mukuka Kapijimpanga elaborated, "On the import side, we rely heavily on machinery, transportation equipment, and consumer goods. This import dependence creates a trade imbalance, especially when copper prices are low. However, diversification into agriculture and non-traditional exports like horticulture, gemstones, and tourism services is helping to mitigate this."

Chanda summarized, "While our trade balance has faced challenges, efforts to diversify exports and reduce import dependency are crucial. Initiatives to boost local manufacturing and value addition in agriculture are steps in the right direction."

Kalenga added, "Furthermore, regional trade agreements within SADC and COMESA open up larger markets for Zambian products, which can improve our trade balance and economic resilience."

Chanda concluded, "Understanding these economic indicators helps us navigate the complexities of our economy and make informed investment decisions. As we continue to explore Zambia's potential, let's keep these insights in mind to build a robust and sustainable economic future."

The session ended with attendees deep in thought, discussing how these economic indicators impacted their areas of interest. The comprehensive overview of Zambia's economic health provided a critical foundation for the subsequent discussions on sector-specific opportunities and strategies.

Investment Climate and Business Environment

The fifth day of the summit had arrived, and the atmosphere was charged with curiosity. Attendees were eager to delve into the practical aspects of investing in Zambia. Chanda Mwamba stood at the podium, ready to discuss the investment climate and business environment.

"Good morning, everyone," Chanda began with a bright smile. "Today, we'll explore the investment climate and business environment in Zambia. We'll cover ease of doing business rankings, major foreign investors, and the challenges and opportunities for investors. Let's get started."

Ease of Doing Business Rankings

Thandiwe Zulu, the financial expert, stepped forward first. "Zambia has made significant strides in improving its ease of doing business rankings. According to the World Bank's Doing Business report, we've seen progress in areas like starting a business, getting credit, and protecting minority investors."

Chanda added, "Indeed, the establishment of the Zambia Development Agency (ZDA) has streamlined business registration processes. What used to take weeks can now be done in days, thanks to the one-stop-shop services provided by the ZDA."

Wamundila Chikumbi chimed in, "However, while we've made progress, there are still areas needing improvement. For instance, dealing with construction permits and accessing electricity can be cumbersome. These are critical areas we need to address to attract more investors."

Major Foreign Investors and Investment Sources

Mutinta Mwiinga spoke next. "Let's talk about major foreign investors. Zambia has attracted significant investments from countries like China, Canada, and South Africa. Chinese investments, particularly in mining and infrastructure, have been substantial. Companies like China Nonferrous Metal Mining Group have invested heavily in our copper mines."

Kalenga Mukuka added, "Canadian companies, such as First Quantum Minerals, have also played a crucial role in the mining sector, bringing in advanced technology and expertise. South African investments are prominent in the retail and banking sectors, with companies like Shoprite and Standard Bank establishing a strong presence here."

Chanda noted, "Additionally, we've seen increasing interest from European and Middle Eastern investors, particularly in the agriculture and energy sectors. These investments are diversifying our economic base and providing new growth opportunities."

Challenges and Opportunities for Investors

Mukuka Kapijimpanga then took the stage. "While Zambia offers numerous opportunities, investors also face challenges. High operational costs, driven by infrastructure deficits and energy shortages, can be a deterrent. Regulatory inconsistencies and bureaucratic red tape are other issues that need addressing."

Thandiwe Zulu pointed out, "Corruption and lack of transparency in some government processes can also be challenging.

However, ongoing reforms aimed at improving governance and accountability are promising steps towards creating a more investor-friendly environment."

Chanda elaborated, "On the opportunities front, Zambia's strategic location as a land-linked country offers significant advantages for regional trade. The development of Special Economic Zones and Industrial Parks provides incentives like tax breaks and duty exemptions, making it attractive for investors to set up operations here."

Mutinta added, "The agriculture sector, with its vast arable land and favorable climate, presents immense opportunities for agribusiness investments. Initiatives to promote value addition and agro-processing are creating new avenues for growth."

Kalenga spoke passionately, "Renewable energy is another sector with high potential. With abundant sunlight and waterways, investments in solar and hydroelectric power can not only meet domestic needs but also position Zambia as an energy exporter in the region."

Chanda concluded, "In summary, while challenges exist, the opportunities in Zambia are vast and varied. By understanding and navigating the investment climate and business environment, we can unlock significant potential and drive sustainable growth."

As the session wrapped up, attendees engaged in lively discussions, sharing their thoughts on the insights provided. The comprehensive overview of Zambia's investment climate and business environment equipped them with valuable knowledge for making informed investment decisions, setting the stage for the summit's remaining sessions focused on sector-specific opportunities.

Future Prospects and Strategic Plans

The final day of the summit had arrived, and there was a palpable sense of excitement in the air. Attendees were eager to hear about the future prospects and strategic plans that would shape Zambia's economic landscape. Chanda Mwamba stood at the podium, ready to lead the discussion.

"Good morning, everyone," Chanda began. "Today, we'll explore Zambia's future prospects and strategic plans. We'll cover Vision 2030, our national development plans, strategic sectors for future investments, and the initiatives from both the government and the private sector. Let's dive in."

Vision 2030 and National Development Plans

Thandiwe Zulu, the financial expert, stepped forward. "Vision 2030 is Zambia's long-term plan to become a prosperous middle-income nation. This vision guides our national development plans, which are designed to achieve sustainable and inclusive growth."

Chanda added, "The current Seventh National Development Plan focuses on economic diversification, job creation, and poverty reduction. It emphasizes sectors like agriculture, tourism, manufacturing, and mining, aiming to reduce our dependence on copper."

Wamundila Chikumbi chimed in, "The plan also includes significant investments in infrastructure, health, and education, recognizing that a strong human capital base is essential for sustained economic growth."

Strategic Sectors for Future Investments

Kalenga Mukuka took the stage. "Strategic sectors for future investments include agriculture, which offers vast potential due to our fertile land and favorable climate. Investments in irrigation, agro-processing, and value addition are critical to unlocking this sector's potential."

Mutinta Mwiinga added, "Tourism is another key sector. Zambia's natural beauty, including the Victoria Falls, national parks, and wildlife, presents immense opportunities for eco-tourism and adventure tourism. Developing infrastructure and promoting sustainable practices will be crucial."

Chanda noted, "Manufacturing is also poised for growth. The establishment of Special Economic Zones and Industrial Parks provides incentives for setting up manufacturing units, which can boost exports and create jobs."

Mukuka Kapijimpanga spoke passionately, "Renewable energy is a sector with significant potential. With abundant sunlight and waterways, investments in solar and hydroelectric power can meet domestic needs and position Zambia as a regional energy exporter."

Government and Private Sector Initiatives

Thandiwe Zulu continued, "The government has launched several initiatives to support these strategic sectors. The establishment of the Zambia Development Agency (ZDA) provides a one-stop shop for investors, offering incentives like tax breaks and duty exemptions."

Chanda added, "The government is also working on improving the business environment by simplifying regulatory procedures, enhancing transparency, and combating corruption. These efforts are crucial for attracting and retaining investments."

Mutinta highlighted, "On the private sector side, there are numerous initiatives aimed at fostering innovation and entrepreneurship. Incubators and accelerators are being established to support startups and SMEs, providing them with the necessary resources to grow and thrive."

Kalenga elaborated, "Public-private partnerships are playing a key role in infrastructure development. Projects like road construction, energy generation, and telecommunications are being undertaken through collaborations between the government and private investors."

Chanda concluded, "In summary, Zambia's future prospects are bright, with strategic plans and initiatives in place to drive sustainable growth. By focusing on key sectors and fostering a conducive investment climate, we can achieve our Vision 2030 goals and build a prosperous future for all Zambians."

As the session ended, the attendees buzzed with excitement, reflecting on the comprehensive overview of Zambia's future prospects and strategic plans. The insights provided a clear roadmap for potential investors, inspiring confidence in Zambia's potential as a thriving investment destination.

2

Chapter 2: Zambia's Booming Sectors

Agriculture and Agribusiness

The sun was shining brightly over the sprawling grounds of the Agricultural Expo in Lusaka. Farmers, investors, and policymakers from across Zambia had gathered to showcase and explore the potential of the country's agricultural sector. Chanda Mwamba, known for his passion for agricultural development, stood at the main stage, ready to highlight Zambia's booming agricultural sector.

"Good morning, everyone," Chanda greeted the enthusiastic crowd. "Today, we are diving into Zambia's thriving agriculture and agribusiness sectors. We'll explore key crops and livestock, agribusiness opportunities, value chains, and the crucial government support and subsidies that drive this dynamic sector forward."

Key Crops and Livestock

Thandiwe Zulu, the agricultural expert, stepped forward. "Let's start with key crops and livestock. Zambia is blessed with fertile soils and diverse agro-ecological zones, making it suitable for a variety of crops and livestock."

Chanda nodded, "Maize is our staple crop, grown across the country and forming the backbone of our agricultural economy. In recent years, there has been a push to diversify into other crops such as wheat, soya beans, and cassava, which are not only for food security but also for export potential."

Mutinta Mwiinga, an agribusiness entrepreneur, added, "Livestock farming, particularly cattle, poultry, and goats, is also significant. These provide meat, dairy products, and contribute to our vibrant livestock industry."

Agribusiness Opportunities and Value Chains

Kalenga Mukuka spoke next, "Agribusiness opportunities abound in Zambia. Beyond primary production, there are opportunities in agro-processing, packaging, and distribution. Value addition along the agricultural value chain is crucial for increasing farm incomes and ensuring food security."

Thandiwe Zulu elaborated, "For example, in the maize value chain, opportunities exist in milling, fortification, and production of maize-based products like cornmeal and breakfast cereals. Similarly, in the horticulture sector, investments in cold storage and transportation can reduce post-harvest losses and expand market reach."

Chanda highlighted, "These value-added activities not only increase profitability but also create employment opportunities along the value chain, from farm to fork."

Government Support and Subsidies

Wamundila Chikumbi, the policy analyst, took the stage. "The government plays a crucial role in supporting agriculture through various policies, subsidies, and incentives. Subsidies for fertilizers, seeds, and mechanization equipment help smallholder farmers improve productivity and income."

Mutinta Mwiinga added, "Government initiatives like the Farmer Input Support Program (FISP) provide subsidized inputs to small-scale farmers, ensuring access to essential agricultural resources. This support is vital for enhancing food security and reducing rural poverty."

Chanda nodded in agreement, "Additionally, the government promotes market linkages and agribusiness development through initiatives like the Rural Finance Expansion Program (RUFEP) and the establishment of agricultural infrastructure such as market hubs and agro-processing zones."

Conclusion

As the session concluded, attendees buzzed with excitement and inspiration. The agricultural expo had not only showcased Zambia's agricultural potential but also highlighted the collaborative efforts between farmers, agribusinesses, and the government to drive sustainable growth.

Chanda looked out at the crowd, filled with optimism. "Zambia's agriculture and agribusiness sectors are not just about farming; they're about building resilient communities, creating jobs, and feeding our nation. Together, we can harness the full potential of this sector and ensure a prosperous future for Zambia."

With that, the crowd applauded, energized by the possibilities ahead. The agricultural sector in Zambia was indeed booming, ready to flourish with innovation, investment, and continued support from all stakeholders.

I apologize for any confusion, but it seems there is a discrepancy in your request. You mentioned continuation of Chapter 1 with point 2, which typically pertains to Chapter 2. Nevertheless, I can generate a continuation of Chapter 2, focusing on Mining and Mineral Resources with the specified subpoints:

Mining and Mineral Resources

The atmosphere in the conference hall in Ndola was charged with anticipation. Industry leaders, investors, and government officials had gathered to discuss Zambia's rich mining and mineral resources sector. Chanda Mwamba, a seasoned geologist and keynote speaker, stood at the podium, ready to unveil the potential of Zambia's mining landscape.

"Good morning, everyone," Chanda greeted the audience warmly. "Today, we will explore Zambia's mining and mineral resources sector, examining major minerals and mining areas, investment opportunities, and crucial environmental and regulatory considerations."

Major Minerals and Mining Areas

Thandiwe Zulu, the mining expert, stepped forward. "Zambia is endowed with abundant mineral resources, with copper being the backbone of our mining sector. The Copperbelt Province, centered around towns like Kitwe and Ndola, remains the heartland of copper mining in Zambia."

Chanda nodded, "In addition to copper, Zambia boasts significant deposits of cobalt, which is often found alongside copper. Cobalt is crucial for industries like battery manufacturing, making Zambia a strategic player in the global cobalt market."

Mutinta Mwiinga, an economist specializing in natural resources, added, "Other minerals of economic importance include emeralds, gold, nickel, and uranium. These minerals are found in various regions across Zambia, presenting diverse opportunities for exploration and development."

Investment Opportunities in Mining

Kalenga Mukuka, a mining engineer with extensive experience, spoke next. "Investment opportunities in Zambia's mining sector are vast. With increasing global demand for minerals, particularly in emerging technologies and renewable energy, Zambia offers favorable conditions for exploration and mining activities."

Thandiwe Zulu elaborated, "The government has implemented policies to attract foreign direct investment (FDI) in the mining sector, including tax incentives, stability agreements, and favorable mining laws. These measures aim to encourage private sector participation and technological advancements in mining operations."

Chanda highlighted, "Furthermore, opportunities exist not only in traditional mining but also in value-added activities such as mineral processing and refining. Investments in these areas can create additional revenue streams and enhance the local economic impact."

Environmental and Regulatory Considerations

Wamundila Chikumbi, a legal expert specializing in environmental law, took the stage. "While mining offers significant economic benefits, it also poses environmental and social challenges. Environmental considerations such as water management, land reclamation, and biodiversity conservation are critical."

Mutinta Mwiinga added, "The government has stringent regulations in place to mitigate these impacts. Environmental impact assessments (EIAs) are mandatory for mining projects, ensuring compliance with environmental standards and promoting sustainable mining practices."

Chanda nodded thoughtfully, "Community engagement and corporate social responsibility (CSR) initiatives are also integral to responsible mining. Companies are encouraged to invest in local communities, supporting education, healthcare, and infrastructure development."

Conclusion

As the session concluded, participants engaged in lively discussions, exchanging insights and exploring potential partnerships. The mining conference had not only highlighted Zambia's rich mineral wealth but also underscored the importance of sustainable practices and collaborative efforts in the mining sector.

Chanda addressed the audience one last time, "Zambia's mining sector is a cornerstone of our economy, driving growth and development. By harnessing our mineral resources responsibly and innovatively, we can create lasting benefits for Zambia and its people."

With renewed enthusiasm, attendees departed, inspired by the possibilities ahead. The future of mining in Zambia looked promising, poised for continued investment, technological advancements, and sustainable development.

Manufacturing and Industrial Development

The bustling forum hall in Lusaka was filled with business leaders, government officials, and potential investors eager to discuss the future of Zambia's manufacturing and industrial development. Chanda Mwamba, a passionate advocate for industrialization, took to the stage to kick off the session.

"Good morning, everyone," Chanda greeted the audience warmly. "Today, we will explore Zambia's manufacturing and industrial development. We'll delve into key industries and industrial zones, manufacturing incentives and policies, and the export potential and markets that are shaping our industrial landscape."

Key Industries and Industrial Zones

Thandiwe Zulu, an industrial development expert, stepped forward. "Zambia has made significant strides in developing key manufacturing industries. Key sectors include food and beverage processing, textiles and garments, chemicals, and construction materials."

Chanda added, "The establishment of Multi-Facility Economic Zones (MFEZs) and industrial parks in Lusaka, Ndola, and other strategic locations has been instrumental in attracting investment and fostering industrial growth. These zones offer modern infrastructure, utilities, and logistical advantages."

Mutinta Mwiinga, an economist with a focus on industrial policy, chimed in, "The Chambishi MFEZ, for instance, has attracted significant investments in copper smelting and manufacturing. Similarly, the Lusaka South MFEZ hosts a variety of industries, from pharmaceuticals to electronics assembly, creating diverse industrial hubs."

Manufacturing Incentives and Policies

Kalenga Mukuka, an investment advisor, spoke next. "To promote manufacturing, the Zambian government has implemented various incentives and policies. These include tax holidays, duty-free importation of capital equipment, and reduced corporate tax rates for businesses operating within MFEZs."

Thandiwe Zulu elaborated, "The government's Industrialization and Job Creation Strategy aims to create an enabling environment for manufacturing by improving infrastructure, enhancing access to finance, and supporting skills development."

Chanda highlighted, "Additionally, the Zambia Development Agency (ZDA) plays a crucial role in facilitating investment and providing support services to manufacturers. The ZDA's one-stop-shop approach simplifies the process of setting up and operating manufacturing businesses."

Export Potential and Markets

Wamundila Chikumbi, a trade expert, took the stage. "Zambia's strategic location as a land-linked country in Southern Africa provides significant export potential. We have access to regional markets through the Southern African Development Community (SADC) and the Common Market for Eastern and Southern Africa (COMESA)."

Mutinta Mwiinga added, "The African Continental Free Trade Area (AfCFTA) also opens up vast opportunities for Zambian manufacturers to access new markets across the continent, promoting intra-African trade."

Chanda noted, "Zambian products, particularly in the agro-processing and textile sectors, are well-positioned for export. By enhancing quality standards and adopting innovative technologies, we can increase our competitiveness in international markets."

Kalenga Mukuka spoke passionately, "Moreover, partnerships with foreign investors and multinational corporations can help Zambian manufacturers integrate into global value chains, further boosting export potential."

Conclusion

As the session concluded, the audience was filled with a renewed sense of optimism about the future of Zambia's manufacturing sector. The forum had provided valuable insights into the key industries, incentives, and export opportunities that are driving industrial development in the country.

Chanda addressed the audience one last time, "Zambia's manufacturing and industrial sector holds immense potential for economic growth and job creation. By leveraging our strategic location, favorable policies, and innovative spirit, we can build a robust and competitive industrial base that benefits all Zambians."

With that, the audience applauded, inspired by the vision of a thriving industrial future for Zambia. The discussions and connections made at the forum would pave the way for new investments, collaborations, and advancements in the manufacturing sector, promising a brighter economic horizon.

Tourism and Hospitality

The majestic Mosi-oa-Tunya, also known as Victoria Falls, provided a breathtaking backdrop for the Tourism Symposium in Livingstone. Attendees from across the globe had gathered to discuss Zambia's tourism and hospitality sector. Chanda Mwamba, a renowned tourism advocate, stood at the podium, ready to guide the discussion.

"Good morning, everyone," Chanda greeted the audience with a warm smile. "Today, we'll explore the vibrant tourism and hospitality sector in Zambia. We'll discuss major tourist attractions, investment opportunities in tourism infrastructure, and the government policies and incentives that support this industry."

Major Tourist Attractions and Destinations

Thandiwe Zulu, an experienced tour operator, stepped forward. "Zambia is a land of stunning natural beauty and diverse wildlife. The Victoria Falls, one of the Seven Natural Wonders of the World, is undoubtedly our most famous attraction, drawing tourists from around the globe."

Chanda nodded, "Beyond the falls, Zambia boasts an array of national parks like South Luangwa, Kafue, and Lower Zambezi. These parks offer unparalleled wildlife experiences, including walking safaris and bird watching, making Zambia a prime destination for eco-tourism."

Mutinta Mwiinga, a cultural heritage expert, added, "Zambia's rich cultural heritage also offers unique tourism experiences. Traditional ceremonies such as the Kuomboka and the N'cwala attract visitors eager to witness and participate in our vibrant cultural traditions."

Investment Opportunities in Tourism Infrastructure

Kalenga Mukuka, a real estate developer specializing in tourism projects, spoke next. "Investment opportunities in Zambia's tourism infrastructure are vast. Developing hotels, lodges, and eco-friendly resorts near major attractions can significantly enhance the tourism experience."

Thandiwe Zulu elaborated, "There's also a growing demand for adventure tourism facilities, such as zip-lining, white-water rafting, and bungee jumping. Investments in these areas can cater to thrill-seekers and boost tourism revenues."

Chanda highlighted, "Improving transportation infrastructure, including airports, roads, and rail links to key tourist destinations, is critical. Enhanced connectivity can attract more visitors and make travel within Zambia more convenient."

Government Policies and Incentives

Wamundila Chikumbi, a policy analyst, took the stage. "The Zambian government is committed to promoting tourism through favorable policies and incentives. The National Tourism Policy outlines strategies to develop and market Zambia as a premier tourist destination."

Mutinta Mwiinga added, "Incentives for investors in the tourism sector include tax holidays, reduced import duties on tourism-related equipment, and land lease options for tourism development. These measures aim to attract both domestic and foreign investment."

Chanda noted, "The government also supports public-private partnerships (PPPs) to develop tourism infrastructure. Collaborations between the government and private sector can lead to the creation of world-class tourism facilities and services."

Kalenga Mukuka spoke passionately, "Furthermore, the Zambia Tourism Agency (ZTA) actively promotes Zambia in international markets through campaigns, trade shows, and partnerships with global travel operators. These efforts help raise Zambia's profile as a must-visit destination."

Conclusion

As the session concluded, the audience buzzed with excitement about the prospects for Zambia's tourism and hospitality sector. The symposium had provided a comprehensive overview of the attractions, investment opportunities, and supportive policies that make Zambia an enticing destination for tourists and investors alike.

Chanda addressed the audience one last time, "Zambia's tourism sector is brimming with potential. By showcasing our natural wonders, cultural heritage, and fostering investment in infrastructure, we can create a thriving tourism industry that benefits both our economy and our communities."

With that, the audience applauded, inspired by the vision of a vibrant and sustainable tourism future for Zambia. The connections made and insights shared at the symposium promised to pave the way for new investments, partnerships, and growth in Zambia's tourism and hospitality sector.

Financial Services and Banking

The grand ballroom of the Lusaka Intercontinental Hotel was abuzz with excitement as financial experts, banking professionals, and investors gathered for the Financial Services Conference. Chanda Mwamba, a well-respected financial consultant, stood at the podium, ready to navigate through the intricacies of Zambia's financial services and banking sector.

"Good morning, everyone," Chanda began, addressing the attentive audience. "Today, we'll delve into Zambia's financial services and banking sector. We'll explore an overview of the banking sector, investment opportunities in financial services, and the regulatory framework and reforms that shape this dynamic industry."

Overview of the Banking Sector

Thandiwe Zulu, a senior economist, stepped forward. "Zambia's banking sector is composed of both local and international banks, providing a range of financial services. Major players include Zambia National Commercial Bank (Zanaco), Standard Chartered, Barclays, and First National Bank (FNB). These institutions offer a variety of products, from savings and loans to complex investment services."

Chanda nodded, "The sector has shown significant growth over the years, driven by technological advancements and increased financial inclusion. Mobile banking and digital payment platforms have expanded access to financial services, especially in rural areas."

Mutinta Mwiinga, a fintech entrepreneur, added, "The rise of fintech companies has revolutionized the banking sector, introducing innovative solutions such as mobile money, online banking, and peer-to-peer lending. These advancements are bridging the gap between the unbanked population and formal financial services."

Investment Opportunities in Financial Services

Kalenga Mukuka, an investment banker, spoke next. "Investment opportunities in Zambia's financial services sector are vast. The growing middle class and increasing adoption of digital banking create a fertile ground for new financial products and services."

Thandiwe Zulu elaborated, "There is significant potential in expanding credit facilities for small and medium-sized enterprises (SMEs). SMEs are the backbone of our economy, and providing them with access to affordable credit can stimulate economic growth and job creation."

Chanda highlighted, "Insurance and microfinance are also promising areas for investment. With a large portion of the population still underserved by traditional financial institutions, there is an opportunity to develop tailored insurance products and microfinance solutions that meet the needs of the underbanked."

Mutinta spoke passionately, "Moreover, fintech presents numerous investment opportunities. By leveraging technology, investors can introduce innovative financial solutions that enhance efficiency, reduce costs, and improve customer experiences."

Regulatory Framework and Reforms

Wamundila Chikumbi, a legal expert specializing in financial regulations, took the stage. "The regulatory framework governing Zambia's financial services sector is robust, ensuring stability and transparency. The Bank of Zambia (BoZ) serves as the central regulatory authority, overseeing banks and financial institutions."

Mutinta Mwiinga added, "Recent reforms have aimed at strengthening the financial sector. These include measures to enhance cybersecurity, promote digital banking, and improve consumer protection. The Financial Sector Development Plan (FSDP) outlines strategies to modernize the sector and foster financial inclusion."

Chanda noted, "The introduction of the National Financial Inclusion Strategy (NFIS) has been a significant step towards increasing access to financial services. The strategy focuses on expanding digital financial services, enhancing financial literacy, and developing supportive regulatory frameworks."

Kalenga Mukuka emphasized, "Compliance with international standards, such as the Basel III regulations, has been prioritized to ensure the stability and resilience of the banking sector. These reforms help build investor confidence and attract foreign direct investment."

Conclusion

As the session concluded, the audience was energized by the insights into Zambia's financial services and banking sector. The conference had highlighted the sector's growth, investment potential, and the regulatory landscape that supports its development.

Chanda addressed the audience one last time, "Zambia's financial services sector is a cornerstone of our economic growth. By fostering innovation, expanding access, and ensuring robust regulatory frameworks, we can create a dynamic and inclusive financial ecosystem that drives prosperity for all Zambians."

With that, the audience applauded, inspired by the vision of a thriving financial services sector in Zambia. The discussions and connections made at the conference promised to pave the way for new investments, partnerships, and advancements in the financial industry, ensuring a stable and prosperous future.

Telecommunications and ICT

The state-of-the-art Lusaka Convention Center was bustling with excitement as tech enthusiasts, entrepreneurs, and investors gathered for the annual ICT Summit. Chanda Mwamba, a prominent technology advocate and keynote speaker, stood at the podium, ready to guide the audience through the dynamic telecommunications and ICT sector in Zambia.

"Good morning, everyone," Chanda began, with a bright smile. "Today, we'll explore Zambia's rapidly growing telecommunications and ICT sector. We'll discuss the growth of the telecom sector, ICT infrastructure development, and the exciting opportunities in digital services and innovations."

Growth of the Telecom Sector

Thandiwe Zulu, a telecommunications expert, stepped forward. "Zambia's telecom sector has experienced remarkable growth over the past decade. The liberalization of the telecom market has led to increased competition and significant improvements in service quality and coverage."

Chanda added, "Major telecom players such as Zamtel, MTN, and Airtel have expanded their networks, providing mobile and internet services to even the most remote areas of the country. This has facilitated greater connectivity and access to information for millions of Zambians."

Mutinta Mwiinga, a digital economy specialist, chimed in, "The advent of 4G and the impending rollout of 5G networks promise to revolutionize the telecom landscape further. Faster and more reliable internet connectivity will enable a host of new services and applications, driving economic growth and innovation."

ICT Infrastructure Development

Kalenga Mukuka, an ICT infrastructure developer, spoke next. "The development of ICT infrastructure is crucial for supporting the growth of the digital economy. Investments in fiber optic networks, data centers, and satellite communication systems are expanding the country's digital backbone."

Thandiwe Zulu elaborated, "Public-private partnerships (PPPs) have been instrumental in accelerating infrastructure projects. For instance, the partnership between the government and private companies has led to the expansion of the national fiber optic network, enhancing connectivity and reducing internet costs."

Chanda highlighted, "Additionally, the establishment of tech hubs and innovation centers, such as the Lusaka Innovation Hub, provides a collaborative space for startups and entrepreneurs to develop and scale their digital solutions. These hubs are crucial for nurturing a vibrant tech ecosystem."

Opportunities in Digital Services and Innovations

Wamundila Chikumbi, a tech entrepreneur, took the stage. "Opportunities in digital services and innovations are vast. The rise of e-commerce platforms, fintech solutions, and e-government services are transforming how businesses and citizens interact with technology."

Mutinta Mwiinga added, "Fintech, in particular, has seen explosive growth. Mobile money services like MTN Mobile Money and Airtel Money have become integral to financial inclusion, allowing people to transfer money, pay bills, and access credit through their mobile phones."

Chanda noted, "E-health and e-education are also burgeoning fields. Digital platforms for healthcare delivery and online learning are expanding access to essential services, especially in rural and underserved areas."

Kalenga Mukuka spoke passionately, "The innovation landscape is further enriched by startups developing cutting-edge solutions in areas such as artificial intelligence, blockchain, and Internet of Things (IoT). These innovations have the potential to address local challenges and position Zambia as a tech hub in the region."

Conclusion

As the session concluded, the audience buzzed with enthusiasm about the future of Zambia's telecommunications and ICT sector. The summit had highlighted the sector's growth, infrastructure developments, and the myriad opportunities for digital innovation and services.

Chanda addressed the audience one last time, "Zambia's telecommunications and ICT sector is a driving force behind our nation's progress. By fostering an environment that encourages innovation, infrastructure development, and digital inclusion, we can harness the power of technology to build a prosperous and connected Zambia."

With that, the audience applauded, inspired by the vision of a thriving digital future for Zambia. The connections made and insights shared at the summit promised to pave the way for new investments, partnerships, and advancements in the ICT sector, ensuring a technologically advanced and inclusive society.

3

Chapter 3: Infrastructure Developments in Zambia

Transportation Network: Roads, Railways, and Aviation

The grand hall of the Lusaka International Conference Center was filled with a mix of government officials, international investors, and local business leaders, all gathered for the Infrastructure Development Summit. The topic on the agenda was the ambitious expansion and modernization of Zambia's transportation network. Chanda Mwamba, an influential figure in infrastructure development, stood at the podium, ready to lead the discussion.

"Good morning, everyone," Chanda began, his voice carrying a tone of optimism and authority. "Today, we'll explore Zambia's transportation network, focusing on major road networks and development projects, railway infrastructure and investment opportunities, and the aviation industry and airport developments. These sectors are critical to our economic growth and connectivity."

Major Road Networks and Development Projects

Thandiwe Zulu, an experienced civil engineer, stepped forward. "Zambia's road network is the backbone of our transportation system. The Great North Road, which connects Lusaka to the northern provinces and beyond, is a vital artery for trade and mobility."

Chanda added, "Recent development projects have focused on upgrading and expanding major highways. The Link Zambia 8000 project aims to create over 8,000 kilometers of road networks, improving connectivity between major cities and rural areas."

Mutinta Mwiinga, a project manager with a focus on infrastructure, elaborated, "The Lusaka-Ndola dual carriageway is one of the flagship projects under this initiative. This highway is crucial for facilitating the movement of goods and people, reducing travel time, and enhancing road safety."

Railway Infrastructure and Investment Opportunities

Kalenga Mukuka, a railway consultant, spoke next. "Zambia's railway network, historically significant, is undergoing revitalization to support our growing economy. The Tanzania-Zambia Railway Authority (TAZARA) and Zambia Railways Limited are central to our rail infrastructure."

Thandiwe Zulu highlighted, "Investment opportunities abound in the railway sector. Modernizing the existing network, expanding rail links to new mining areas, and developing freight corridors are key areas of focus."

Chanda nodded, "The North-South Corridor project aims to enhance rail connectivity between Zambia and its neighbors, facilitating regional trade. By improving rail infrastructure, we can reduce the cost of transporting bulk goods and support sustainable economic growth."

Mutinta added passionately, "Public-private partnerships are essential for advancing our railway infrastructure. Collaborations between the government and private investors can bring in the necessary capital and expertise to drive these projects forward."

Aviation Industry and Airport Developments

Wamundila Chikumbi, an aviation expert, took the stage. "The aviation industry in Zambia is experiencing significant growth, with investments in airport infrastructure and services. Kenneth Kaunda International Airport in Lusaka is our main gateway, and its expansion is a testament to our commitment to modernizing aviation facilities."

Mutinta Mwiinga elaborated, "The new passenger terminal at Kenneth Kaunda International Airport, with its increased capacity and modern amenities, positions Lusaka as a regional hub for air travel. This development not only enhances passenger experience but also boosts cargo handling capabilities."

Chanda highlighted, "Other airports, such as Simon Mwansa Kapwepwe International Airport in Ndola and Harry Mwanga Nkumbula International Airport in Livingstone, are also undergoing upgrades. These improvements are essential for accommodating increasing air traffic and supporting tourism and business travel."

Kalenga Mukuka emphasized, "Investment opportunities in the aviation sector extend beyond airports. Developing aviation-related services, such as maintenance, repair, and overhaul (MRO) facilities, and enhancing domestic flight connectivity are critical for supporting the broader economic goals."

Conclusion

As the session concluded, the audience was energized by the comprehensive overview of Zambia's transportation network. The summit had provided valuable insights into the road, rail, and aviation sectors, highlighting ongoing projects, investment opportunities, and the transformative impact of infrastructure development.

Chanda addressed the audience one last time, "Zambia's transportation network is the lifeline of our economy. By investing in roads, railways, and aviation infrastructure, we are building the foundation for sustainable growth, regional integration, and improved quality of life for all Zambians."

With that, the audience applauded, inspired by the vision of a connected and prosperous Zambia. The discussions and connections made at the summit promised to pave the way for new investments, partnerships, and advancements in the transportation sector, ensuring a robust and integrated infrastructure network for the future.

Energy and Power Generation

The Lusaka Energy Conference was abuzz with anticipation as industry experts, policymakers, and investors gathered to discuss Zambia's energy sector. The ballroom was filled with displays showcasing the latest in energy technology and innovations. Chanda Mwamba, a respected energy analyst, took the stage, ready to delve into the current state and future prospects of Zambia's energy and power generation landscape.

"Good morning, everyone," Chanda began, addressing the eager audience. "Today, we'll explore Zambia's energy and power generation sector. Our discussion will cover the current energy mix and power generation capacity, renewable energy opportunities, and the government policies and incentives that drive this vital industry."

Current Energy Mix and Power Generation Capacity

Thandiwe Zulu, an energy sector veteran, stepped forward. "Zambia's energy mix is predominantly hydroelectric, accounting for over 80% of our power generation. Major hydroelectric plants like the Kariba North Bank, Kafue Gorge, and Victoria Falls contribute significantly to our capacity."

Chanda added, "While our reliance on hydro power has provided a renewable source of energy, it also makes us vulnerable to climate variability. Periods of drought have led to significant power shortages, highlighting the need for diversification in our energy mix."

Mutinta Mwiinga, a power generation engineer, elaborated, "Our total installed power generation capacity stands at around 2,800 MW. However, due to aging infrastructure and maintenance challenges, the actual available capacity is often lower. To address this, ongoing projects aim to upgrade and expand existing facilities."

Renewable Energy Opportunities

Kalenga Mukuka, a renewable energy entrepreneur, spoke next. "There is immense potential for renewable energy in Zambia. Solar power, in particular, is a promising resource given our high solar irradiance. Projects like the Bangweulu and Ngonye solar plants are already making strides in harnessing this potential."

Thandiwe Zulu highlighted, "Wind and geothermal energy are also areas with significant untapped potential. Feasibility studies and pilot projects are underway to explore these options, which could further diversify our energy mix and enhance energy security."

Chanda nodded, "Additionally, biomass and small-scale hydro projects offer viable solutions for rural electrification. These projects can provide off-grid communities with access to reliable and sustainable energy, supporting local development and improving livelihoods."

Mutinta spoke passionately, "Investment opportunities in the renewable energy sector are vast. From solar farms to wind turbines, there is a growing demand for clean energy solutions. Private sector involvement, along with international partnerships, is crucial for scaling up these initiatives."

Government Policies and Incentives for Energy Sector

Wamundila Chikumbi, a policy advisor, took the stage. "The Zambian government has implemented several policies and incentives to attract investment in the energy sector. The National Energy Policy aims to ensure a secure, reliable, and affordable energy supply through diversification and infrastructure development."

Mutinta Mwiinga added, "Incentives such as tax breaks, feed-in tariffs, and duty exemptions on renewable energy equipment are designed to encourage private sector participation. The Renewable Energy Feed-in Tariff (REFiT) strategy, for instance, provides guaranteed pricing for electricity generated from renewable sources."

Chanda highlighted, "The Energy Regulation Board (ERB) plays a crucial role in overseeing and regulating the sector, ensuring fair practices and promoting transparency. Additionally, the Rural Electrification Authority (REA) focuses on expanding access to electricity in remote areas, aligning with the government's goal of achieving universal access to electricity by 2030."

Kalenga Mukuka emphasized, "Public-private partnerships are essential for advancing large-scale energy projects. Collaborations between the government, local businesses, and international investors can bring in the necessary expertise and capital to drive these projects forward."

Conclusion

As the session concluded, the audience was invigorated by the comprehensive overview of Zambia's energy sector. The conference had highlighted the current energy mix, the vast potential of renewable energy, and the supportive policies and incentives that make Zambia an attractive destination for energy investments.

Chanda addressed the audience one last time, "Zambia's

energy sector is at a pivotal point. By diversifying our energy sources, investing in renewable technologies, and fostering a supportive policy environment, we can build a resilient and sustainable energy future for our nation."

With that, the audience applauded, inspired by the vision of a greener and more reliable energy sector in Zambia. The discussions and connections made at the conference promised to pave the way for new investments, partnerships, and advancements in the energy sector, ensuring a bright and sustainable future.

Information and Communication Technology

The National ICT Summit was in full swing at the Mulungushi International Conference Centre. Attendees, including tech entrepreneurs, government officials, and international investors, filled the grand hall. Excitement buzzed in the air as they prepared to delve into Zambia's ICT landscape. Chanda Mwamba, a renowned ICT advocate, took the podium to begin the session.

"Good morning, everyone," Chanda greeted the audience warmly. "Today, we'll be exploring Zambia's ICT sector. Our discussion will cover ICT infrastructure and internet penetration, government incentives in ICT development, and opportunities in tech startups and innovation hubs. Let's dive into how we're transforming Zambia into a digital powerhouse."

ICT Infrastructure and Internet Penetration

Thandiwe Zulu, an ICT infrastructure specialist, stepped forward. "Zambia's ICT infrastructure has seen substantial growth in recent years. The expansion of fiber optic networks and mobile broadband services has significantly improved internet connectivity across the country."

Chanda added, "Currently, internet penetration stands at around 40%, with significant strides being made to increase this figure. Projects like the Smart Zambia Initiative aim to provide widespread internet access, especially in rural and underserved areas."

Mutinta Mwiinga, a digital inclusion advocate, elaborated, "Mobile network operators like MTN, Airtel, and Zamtel have played a crucial role in enhancing connectivity. The rollout of 4G LTE networks and the planned introduction of 5G services promise to further boost internet speeds and accessibility."

Government Incentives in ICT Development

Kalenga Mukuka, a policy expert, spoke next. "The Zambian government recognizes the transformative potential of ICT and has implemented various incentives to encourage development in this sector. The National ICT Policy outlines strategies to create a conducive environment for ICT growth."

Thandiwe Zulu highlighted, "Incentives include tax breaks and subsidies for ICT companies, as well as grants for research and development in technology. The government also supports public-private partnerships to drive large-scale ICT projects."

Chanda nodded, "The creation of the Ministry of Communications and Transport, along with agencies like the

Zambia Information and Communications Technology Authority (ZICTA), underscores the government's commitment to regulating and promoting the ICT sector effectively."

Mutinta added, "Programs like the Universal Access Fund are aimed at bridging the digital divide by funding ICT projects in rural areas. This ensures that all Zambians, regardless of their location, can benefit from digital advancements."

Opportunities in Tech Startups and Innovation Hubs

Wamundila Chikumbi, a tech entrepreneur, took the stage. "Zambia's tech startup ecosystem is burgeoning, with numerous opportunities for innovation and investment. Innovation hubs like BongoHive in Lusaka provide a collaborative space for startups to grow and thrive."

Mutinta Mwiinga elaborated, "These hubs offer mentorship, training, and funding opportunities for young entrepreneurs. They play a critical role in nurturing talent and fostering a culture of innovation."

Chanda highlighted, "Sectors such as fintech, e-commerce, and health tech are particularly promising. With the rise of mobile money services and digital payment platforms, fintech startups are revolutionizing the financial landscape."

Kalenga Mukuka spoke passionately, "E-commerce platforms are transforming retail, enabling businesses to reach a wider audience and providing consumers with greater convenience. Additionally, health tech innovations are improving access to healthcare services, particularly in remote areas."

Conclusion

As the session concluded, the audience was energized by the insights into Zambia's ICT sector. The summit had highlighted the significant strides in ICT infrastructure, the supportive government policies, and the vast opportunities for tech startups and innovation.

Chanda addressed the audience one last time, "Zambia's ICT sector is a beacon of potential and progress. By investing in infrastructure, fostering innovation, and supporting tech startups, we can build a digitally inclusive and technologically advanced nation."

With that, the audience applauded, inspired by the vision of a connected and innovative Zambia. The discussions and connections made at the summit promised to pave the way for new investments, partnerships, and advancements in the ICT sector, ensuring a robust digital future for all Zambians.

Water Supply and Sanitation

The Lusaka National Water Supply and Sanitation Forum was underway at the Taj Pamodzi Hotel. The event drew a diverse crowd of government officials, international donors, private sector leaders, and NGOs, all focused on addressing Zambia's water and sanitation challenges. Chanda Mwamba, a well-respected environmental engineer, stood at the podium, ready to lead the discussion.

"Good morning, everyone," Chanda began, her voice steady and clear. "Today, we'll be examining Zambia's water supply and sanitation sector. We'll discuss the current water supply infrastructure, investment opportunities in water and sanitation, and government policies and public-private partnerships that are crucial for the sector's development."

Current Water Supply Infrastructure

Thandiwe Zulu, a senior engineer with the Lusaka Water and Sewerage Company, stepped forward. "Zambia's water supply infrastructure has seen improvements, but challenges remain, particularly in rural areas. Urban centers like Lusaka and Ndola have relatively better access to potable water, but infrastructure is aging and in need of upgrades."

Chanda added, "Rural areas still face significant difficulties in accessing clean water. Many communities rely on boreholes and wells, which are often inadequately maintained. The government has been working on programs to expand and improve water supply systems, but there is a long way to go."

Mutinta Mwiinga, a community development expert, elaborated, "The situation in rural areas underscores the need for robust infrastructure. Projects like the Integrated Small Towns Water Supply and Sanitation Program aim to improve access in peri-urban and rural settings by constructing new water supply systems and rehabilitating existing ones."

Investment Opportunities in Water and Sanitation

Kalenga Mukuka, an investment analyst, spoke next. "The water and sanitation sector presents numerous investment opportunities. With a growing population and urbanization, the demand for improved water services is increasing. There is a substantial need for private investment to bridge the infrastructure gap."

Thandiwe Zulu highlighted, "Opportunities exist in various areas such as water treatment facilities, pipeline construction, and wastewater management. Innovative technologies like desalination and rainwater harvesting systems also offer potential solutions."

Chanda nodded, "Sanitation is equally critical. Investment in modern sewage treatment plants and decentralized sanitation systems can greatly improve public health and environmental conditions. There is also a growing market for products and services that promote hygiene and sanitation."

Mutinta added passionately, "Investors can also look into public-private partnerships (PPPs), which are instrumental in mobilizing resources and expertise for large-scale projects. These partnerships can ensure sustainable development and efficient service delivery."

Government Policies and Public-Private Partnerships

Wamundila Chikumbi, a policy advisor from the Ministry of Water Development, Sanitation and Environmental Protection, took the stage. "The Zambian government has implemented several policies to attract investment and promote sustainable water and sanitation services. The National Water Policy and the Seventh National Development Plan emphasize the importance of water security and sanitation."

Mutinta Mwiinga elaborated, "Government policies aim to create an enabling environment for private sector participation. Incentives such as tax exemptions for water infrastructure projects and streamlined regulatory processes are designed to attract investors."

Chanda highlighted, "The government has also been fostering PPPs to address the sector's challenges. Successful examples include the Lusaka Sanitation Project, which combines public funds with private expertise to upgrade the city's sewage system and improve sanitation services."

Kalenga Mukuka emphasized, "International partnerships are also crucial. Organizations like the World Bank, African Development Bank, and UNICEF have been pivotal in funding and supporting water and sanitation projects in Zambia. These collaborations are vital for scaling up efforts and achieving long-term sustainability."

Conclusion

As the session concluded, the audience felt a renewed sense of commitment to improving Zambia's water supply and sanitation sector. The forum had provided valuable insights into the current infrastructure, investment opportunities, and supportive government policies and partnerships.

Chanda addressed the audience one last time, "Zambia's water supply and sanitation sector is essential for the health and well-being of our citizens. By investing in infrastructure, fostering public-private partnerships, and supporting innovative solutions, we can ensure access to clean water and improved sanitation for all Zambians."

With that, the audience applauded, inspired by the vision of a future where clean water and effective sanitation are accessible to everyone. The discussions and connections made at the forum promised to pave the way for new investments, partnerships, and advancements in the sector, ensuring a healthier and more sustainable Zambia.

Housing and Real Estate Development

The conference hall at the Lusaka Real Estate Investment Forum buzzed with energy as developers, investors, and government officials gathered to discuss the burgeoning opportunities in Zambia's housing and real estate market. Among the attendees were Chanda Mwamba, a seasoned real estate developer; Mutinta Mwiinga, an aspiring property investor; and Wamundila Chikumbi, an urban planner passionate about sustainable development.

Urbanization Trends and Housing Demand

Chanda Mwamba took the stage first, her presentation highlighting the rapid urbanization trends in Zambia. "Lusaka and other major cities are experiencing unprecedented urban growth," she began. "With the urban population expected to double in the next decade, the demand for affordable housing is at an all-time high. This presents a significant opportunity for real estate development."

Mutinta, seated in the front row, nodded thoughtfully, making notes on the potential market for mid-range housing developments.

Investment Opportunities in Real Estate

Next, Wamundila Chikumbi shared insights on investment opportunities in the sector. "The real estate market in Zambia is ripe for investment," he said. "From residential housing to commercial properties and mixed-use developments, the opportunities are vast. The government's focus on improving urban infrastructure further enhances the attractiveness of real estate investments."

He continued, "Projects like the Lusaka Decongestion Project and various road network improvements are set to increase the value of real estate in these areas. Investors should look at emerging neighborhoods and upcoming infrastructure projects as key areas for development."

Regulatory Framework for Real Estate Development

Finally, Chanda returned to discuss the regulatory framework. "Navigating the regulatory environment is crucial for successful real estate development," she emphasized. "The government has introduced several reforms to streamline the approval process and make it easier for developers to obtain necessary permits and licenses. Understanding zoning laws, land acquisition processes, and building codes is essential."

She added, "Collaborating with local authorities and staying updated on policy changes can help mitigate risks and ensure compliance. The Ministry of Lands and Natural Resources, along with local councils, play a pivotal role in regulating real estate activities."

Conclusion

As the session concluded, Mutinta and Wamundila engaged in a lively discussion, exploring potential collaborations and strategies to capitalize on the opportunities presented. They left the forum inspired, armed with knowledge about urbanization trends, investment opportunities, and the regulatory framework necessary to thrive in Zambia's dynamic real estate market.

Chanda's final words echoed in their minds: "Zambia's housing and real estate sector is not just about bricks and mortar; it's about building communities and creating sustainable urban environments for future generations. Together, we can shape the future of Zambia's cities and unlock the full potential of the real estate market."

Logistics and Supply Chain Infrastructure

The National Logistics and Supply Chain Conference was abuzz with industry professionals, government officials, and international stakeholders at the luxurious Royal Livingstone Hotel. Against the backdrop of Victoria Falls, Chanda Mwamba, a seasoned logistics expert, took the stage to lead discussions on Zambia's logistics and supply chain infrastructure.

"Good morning, esteemed guests," Chanda greeted the audience, her voice echoing in the conference hall. "Today, we'll delve into Zambia's logistics and supply chain infrastructure. Our focus will be on the overview of the sectors, investment opportunities in logistics infrastructure, and government policies and support measures. Let's explore how Zambia is enhancing its logistical capabilities to drive economic growth."

Overview of Logistics and Supply Chain Sectors

Thandiwe Zulu, a logistics analyst, stepped forward. "Zambia's logistics sector plays a pivotal role in facilitating trade and economic activities. With its strategic location in Southern Africa and well-established transport networks, the country serves as a gateway for regional and international commerce."

Chanda added, "The logistics industry encompasses a wide range of activities, including transportation, warehousing, freight forwarding, and distribution. Efficient logistics and supply chain management are crucial for reducing costs, improving delivery times, and enhancing overall competitiveness."

Mutinta Mwiinga, a supply chain management consultant, elaborated, "The development of logistics infrastructure supports various sectors, from agriculture and mining to manufacturing and retail. Integrated supply chains ensure that goods move swiftly and efficiently across the country and beyond."

Investment Opportunities in Logistics Infrastructure

Kalenga Mukuka, an investment advisor, spoke next. "Zambia offers numerous investment opportunities in logistics infrastructure. The expansion and modernization of road networks, railways, and ports are key areas of focus. Projects such as the Lusaka-Ndola Dual Carriageway and the rehabilitation of the TAZARA railway are examples of initiatives aimed at enhancing connectivity and reducing transport costs."

Thandiwe Zulu highlighted, "Investments in warehousing facilities and logistics parks are also critical. With the growth of e-commerce and retail sectors, there is a rising demand for modern storage and distribution centers that can efficiently handle goods and manage inventory."

Chanda nodded, "Moreover, advancements in technology, such as GPS tracking systems and digital platforms for logistics management, present opportunities for innovation and efficiency gains in the sector. These technologies enable real-time monitoring of shipments, optimizing routes, and reducing operational costs."

Government Policies and Support Measures

Wamundila Chikumbi, a policy expert from the Ministry of Transport and Communications, took the stage. "The Zambian government has implemented several policies and support measures to enhance the logistics and supply chain infrastructure. The National Transport Policy and the Seventh National Development Plan prioritize infrastructure development to support economic growth."

Mutinta Mwiinga elaborated, "Government initiatives include regulatory reforms to streamline customs procedures and reduce bureaucratic hurdles. These reforms aim to improve the ease of doing business and attract private sector investments in logistics."

Chanda highlighted, "The Zambia Revenue Authority (ZRA) has introduced initiatives such as the Electronic Cargo Tracking System (ECTS) to combat transit fraud and ensure the security of cargo in transit. Such measures contribute to a more secure and reliable logistics environment."

Kalenga Mukuka emphasized, "Public-private partnerships (PPPs) are instrumental in mobilizing resources for large-scale infrastructure projects. The government collaborates with private sector entities to fund, develop, and manage critical logistics facilities and services."

Conclusion

As the session concluded, the audience felt invigorated by the potential of Zambia's logistics and supply chain sector. The conference had provided valuable insights into the sectors, showcased investment opportunities, and highlighted the supportive government policies and measures.

Chanda addressed the audience one last time, "Zambia's logistics and supply chain infrastructure are fundamental to its economic development. By investing in modern infrastructure, leveraging technology, and fostering partnerships, we can create a seamless and efficient logistics network that supports sustainable growth and prosperity."

With that, the audience applauded, inspired by the vision of a robust logistics sector driving Zambia forward. The discussions and connections made at the conference promised to pave the way for new investments, partnerships, and advancements in logistics and supply chain infrastructure, ensuring Zambia's continued integration into regional and global supply networks.

4

Chapter 4: Government Incentives for Investors

Special Economic Zones and Industrial Parks

The National Investment Conference was in full swing at the prestigious Mulungushi International Conference Center in Lusaka. Government officials, investors, and business leaders from around the world gathered to explore opportunities in Zambia's Special Economic Zones (SEZs) and Industrial Parks. Chanda Mwamba, a distinguished economist, took the stage to highlight the government's initiatives and incentives for attracting investment through SEZs and Industrial Parks.

"Good morning, esteemed guests," Chanda greeted the audience warmly. "Today, we will delve into Zambia's Special Economic Zones and Industrial Parks. Our discussion will cover an overview of SEZs, the benefits and incentives they offer, and success stories from established zones. Let us explore how these initiatives are fostering economic growth and attracting investment to Zambia."

Overview of Special Economic Zones (SEZs)

Thandiwe Zulu, a senior official from the Zambia Development Agency (ZDA), stepped forward. "Special Economic Zones are designated geographical areas within Zambia that offer unique incentives and a supportive business environment to attract both domestic and foreign investments. These zones are strategically located and equipped with infrastructure to facilitate specific economic activities."

Chanda added, "SEZs aim to stimulate industrialization, boost exports, create employment opportunities, and promote technology transfer and innovation. They typically offer streamlined administrative procedures, tax incentives, and regulatory frameworks tailored to meet the needs of businesses operating within them."

Benefits and Incentives for SEZs

Kalenga Mukuka, an investment advisor, spoke next. "SEZs in Zambia offer a range of benefits and incentives to investors. These include tax holidays on corporate income tax, exemptions from import duties and VAT on machinery and equipment, and reduced or waived customs duties on raw materials and intermediate goods."

Thandiwe Zulu highlighted, "Other incentives include simplified customs procedures, allowing for faster clearance of goods, and access to reliable infrastructure such as roads, electricity, and water supply. These incentives significantly lower the cost of doing business and enhance the competitiveness of companies operating within SEZs."

Success Stories and Case Studies

Mutinta Mwiinga, a business development consultant, took the floor. "Zambia has witnessed notable success stories from its SEZs. One such example is the Lusaka South Multi-Facility Economic Zone (LS-MFEZ), which has attracted investments in manufacturing, agribusiness, and logistics sectors."

Chanda nodded, "LS-MFEZ has become a hub for companies looking to capitalize on Zambia's strategic location and conducive business environment. The zone has created thousands of jobs, facilitated technology transfer, and contributed significantly to the country's export earnings."

Mutinta added passionately, "Another success story is the MFEZ in Ndola, which focuses on heavy industries such as mining equipment manufacturing and assembly. This zone has not only attracted international investors but has also stimulated local industrial growth and skills development."

Conclusion

As the session concluded, the audience felt inspired by Zambia's commitment to fostering investment through SEZs and Industrial Parks. The conference had provided valuable insights into the benefits, incentives, and success stories of these economic zones, highlighting their pivotal role in driving economic diversification and sustainable growth.

Chanda addressed the audience one last time, "Special Economic Zones and Industrial Parks represent a cornerstone of Zambia's investment strategy. By providing a conducive business environment, attractive incentives, and robust infrastructure, we aim to attract more investments, stimulate industrialization, and create prosperity for all Zambians."

With that, the audience applauded, energized by the opportunities presented through SEZs and Industrial Parks. The discussions and connections made at the conference promised to pave the way for new investments, partnerships, and advancements in Zambia's economic landscape, ensuring continued growth and development for years to come.

Tax Incentives and Duty Exemptions

The Investor Workshop at the Zambia Revenue Authority (ZRA) Headquarters was bustling with activity. Potential investors, government representatives, and business consultants gathered to learn about the tax incentives and duty exemptions available to those willing to invest in Zambia. Chanda Mwamba, a prominent tax advisor, stood ready to share her expertise.

"Good morning, everyone," Chanda began, her voice clear and welcoming. "Today, we're going to explore the tax incentives and duty exemptions designed to attract investment in Zambia. We will cover an overview of tax incentives for investors, duty exceptions and reductions, and the application procedures and eligibility criteria. Let's dive into how these incentives can benefit your business ventures in Zambia."

Overview of Tax Incentives for Investors

Thandiwe Zulu, a senior official from the Ministry of Finance, took the floor. "The Zambian government offers a range of tax incentives to encourage investment across various sectors. These incentives are aimed at reducing the cost of doing business and enhancing the profitability of investments."

Chanda added, "Key tax incentives include corporate income tax holidays, accelerated depreciation allowances, and tax credits for investments in certain sectors such as agriculture, manufacturing, and tourism. For instance, companies operating in Multi-Facility Economic Zones (MFEZs) and Industrial Parks can enjoy a tax holiday of up to 10 years."

Mutinta Mwiinga, an accountant specializing in corporate tax, elaborated, "Investors in priority sectors like agriculture and mining can benefit from reduced tax rates on profits and favorable terms for reinvestment. These incentives are designed to stimulate economic activities that contribute to job creation and export growth."

Duty Exceptions and Reductions

Kalenga Mukuka, a customs expert from ZRA, spoke next. "In addition to tax incentives, Zambia offers duty exemptions and reductions to lower the costs of importing essential goods and equipment. These exemptions apply to machinery, equipment, and raw materials used in manufacturing and other productive sectors."

Thandiwe Zulu highlighted, "The duty exemptions also cover imports for projects in priority sectors, including agriculture, tourism, and renewable energy. This makes it more affordable for businesses to set up operations and expand their production capacities."

Chanda nodded, "Duty reductions are available for specific goods that are critical for industrial and infrastructure development. For example, materials used in the construction of industrial plants or renewable energy projects can benefit from significantly reduced import duties."

Mutinta added passionately, "These duty incentives not only reduce the initial capital outlay for investors but also enhance the overall competitiveness of Zambian products in international markets by lowering production costs."

Application Procedures and Eligibility Criteria

Wamundila Chikumbi, a regulatory affairs specialist, took the stage. "To benefit from these tax incentives and duty exemptions, investors must follow specific application procedures and meet eligibility criteria. The ZRA and Zambia Development Agency (ZDA) provide clear guidelines to facilitate this process."

Mutinta Mwiinga elaborated, "The application process typically involves submitting a detailed business plan, financial projections, and evidence of compliance with sector-specific regulations. The ZDA evaluates these applications to ensure they align with national development goals."

Chanda highlighted, "Eligibility criteria vary depending on the type of incentive and the sector of investment. Generally, businesses must demonstrate their potential to create jobs, generate foreign exchange earnings, and contribute to sustainable economic development."

Kalenga Mukuka emphasized, "Investors can seek assistance from the ZRA and ZDA throughout the application process. These agencies offer support services to help businesses navigate the regulatory requirements and maximize the benefits of the available incentives."

Conclusion

As the workshop concluded, the audience felt empowered by the comprehensive overview of Zambia's tax incentives and duty exemptions. The session had provided valuable insights into the benefits, application procedures, and eligibility criteria, highlighting the government's commitment to fostering a conducive investment climate.

Chanda addressed the audience one last time, "Zambia's tax incentives and duty exemptions are designed to attract and support investment in key sectors. By understanding and leveraging these benefits, investors can significantly enhance the viability and profitability of their projects in Zambia."

With that, the audience applauded, inspired by the opportunities presented through the government's incentives. The discussions and connections made at the workshop promised to pave the way for new investments, partnerships, and advancements in Zambia's economic landscape, ensuring continued growth and prosperity for the nation.

Investment Protection and Guarantees

The International Investment Forum was held at the Intercontinental Hotel in Lusaka, attracting investors, legal experts, and government officials from around the world. The conference hall was filled with an air of anticipation as Chanda Mwamba, an expert in international investment law, prepared to discuss the crucial topic of investment protection and guarantees in Zambia.

"Good afternoon, distinguished guests," Chanda began, her voice resonating with confidence. "Today, we will explore the legal framework for investment protection in Zambia, bilateral investment treaties (BITs), and the role of the Zambia Development Agency (ZDA). Let's understand how these mechanisms ensure that investments in Zambia are secure and protected."

Legal Framework for Investment Protection

Thandiwe Zulu, a senior legal advisor from the Ministry of Justice, took the stage. "Zambia has established a robust legal framework to protect investments and ensure a conducive environment for business. The primary legislation governing investment is the Zambia Investment Act, which provides comprehensive protections for investors."

Chanda added, "The Investment Act guarantees against nationalization and expropriation except for public purposes and upon payment of prompt, adequate, and effective compensation. This assurance is crucial for instilling confidence among investors."

Mutinta Mwiinga, a corporate lawyer, elaborated, "The Act also provides for the repatriation of profits, dividends, and capital, ensuring that investors can freely transfer their earnings out of the country. This provision is essential for international investors seeking to protect their financial interests."

Bilateral Investment Treaties (BITs)

Kalenga Mukuka, an international trade expert, spoke next. "Bilateral Investment Treaties (BITs) play a significant role in protecting foreign investments. Zambia has entered into numerous BITs with countries around the world to provide additional legal security to investors."

Thandiwe Zulu highlighted, "These treaties offer protection against unfair treatment, expropriation, and ensure the free transfer of funds. They also provide mechanisms for resolving disputes through international arbitration, which is a key aspect of investor protection."

Chanda nodded, "BITs enhance the legal certainty and predictability for investors by ensuring that their investments are treated fairly and equitably. They serve as a powerful tool in mitigating risks associated with foreign investments."

Mutinta added passionately, "Moreover, BITs foster a favorable investment climate by demonstrating Zambia's commitment to upholding international standards and obligations. This commitment is crucial in attracting long-term investments and fostering economic growth."

Role of the Zambia Development Agency (ZDA)

Wamundila Chikumbi, a senior representative from the Zambia Development Agency (ZDA), took the floor. "The ZDA plays a pivotal role in promoting and facilitating investment in Zambia. Our mandate includes providing comprehensive support to investors and ensuring their interests are protected."

Mutinta Mwiinga elaborated, "The ZDA offers a one-stop-shop service for investors, assisting them with regulatory approvals, permits, and licenses. This streamlined process reduces the bureaucratic burden and accelerates the establishment of business operations."

Chanda highlighted, "The ZDA also provides aftercare services to ensure that investors receive continuous support throughout their investment journey. This includes addressing any challenges they may face and facilitating interactions with various government agencies."

Kalenga Mukuka emphasized, "Additionally, the ZDA actively promotes Zambia as a prime investment destination through international roadshows, investment forums, and marketing campaigns. By showcasing Zambia's investment opportunities and regulatory framework, the ZDA attracts new investors and fosters economic development."

Conclusion

As the session concluded, the audience felt reassured by the comprehensive investment protection and guarantees provided in Zambia. The forum had provided valuable insights into the legal framework, BITs, and the supportive role of the ZDA, highlighting Zambia's commitment to creating a secure and attractive investment climate.

Chanda addressed the audience one last time, "Zambia's investment protection mechanisms are designed to safeguard investor interests and foster a stable and conducive environment for business. By understanding and leveraging these protections, investors can confidently pursue opportunities in Zambia, contributing to the nation's economic growth and development."

With that, the audience applauded, inspired by the robust protections and guarantees offered to investors. The discussions and connections made at the forum promised to pave the way for new investments, partnerships, and advancements in

Zambia's economic landscape, ensuring continued growth and prosperity for the nation.

Grants and Subsidies

The Economic Development Seminar was held at the Radisson Blu Hotel in Lusaka, attracting investors, business leaders, and policy makers. The seminar room buzzed with conversations about the latest opportunities in Zambia's evolving economic landscape. Chanda Mwamba, a renowned economic development expert, prepared to share insights on the government grants and subsidies available to investors.

"Good afternoon, everyone," Chanda began, her voice filled with enthusiasm. "Today, we're going to discuss the various grants and subsidies offered by the Zambian government to support strategic sectors. We'll cover government grants for strategic sectors, subsidy programs and their impact, and the eligibility and application process. Let's explore how these incentives can help fuel your business ventures in Zambia."

Government Grants for Strategic Sectors

Thandiwe Zulu, a senior official from the Ministry of Commerce, Trade, and Industry, took the floor. "The Zambian government offers targeted grants to encourage investment in strategic sectors crucial for economic growth. These sectors include agriculture, renewable energy, manufacturing, and tourism."

Chanda added, "Government grants are designed to support

projects that align with national development goals. For instance, in the agriculture sector, grants are provided to farmers and agribusinesses to improve productivity, enhance value chains, and support sustainable farming practices."

Mutinta Mwiinga, an agribusiness consultant, elaborated, "In renewable energy, grants are available for projects that develop solar, wind, and hydroelectric power. These grants aim to increase the country's energy capacity, reduce reliance on fossil fuels, and promote green energy solutions."

Subsidy Programs and Their Impact

Kalenga Mukuka, an economic policy analyst, spoke next. "Subsidy programs play a significant role in lowering the cost of production and increasing the competitiveness of local businesses. These programs are particularly impactful in sectors like agriculture and manufacturing."

Thandiwe Zulu highlighted, "Agricultural subsidies help farmers access essential inputs such as fertilizers, seeds, and equipment at reduced costs. This support boosts agricultural productivity, enhances food security, and increases export potential."

Chanda nodded, "In the manufacturing sector, subsidies on raw materials and machinery reduce production costs, enabling manufacturers to produce goods more competitively. This leads to increased industrial output, job creation, and economic diversification."

Mutinta added passionately, "The impact of these subsidies extends beyond individual businesses. They stimulate economic activity, create employment opportunities, and contribute to overall economic growth. By supporting key industries, subsidies help build a resilient and diversified economy."

Eligibility and Application Process

Wamundila Chikumbi, a senior representative from the Zambia Development Agency (ZDA), took the stage. "Eligibility for government grants and subsidies depends on the alignment of the proposed projects with national development priorities. Applicants must demonstrate the potential economic and social benefits of their projects."

Mutinta Mwiinga elaborated, "The application process involves submitting a detailed project proposal, including financial projections, business plans, and evidence of compliance with relevant regulations. The ZDA evaluates these applications to ensure they meet the eligibility criteria and contribute to strategic sectors."

Chanda highlighted, "Applicants can seek assistance from the ZDA and other government agencies throughout the application process. These bodies provide guidance on preparing proposals, navigating regulatory requirements, and maximizing the chances of securing grants and subsidies."

Kalenga Mukuka emphasized, "The ZDA also offers support services such as workshops and advisory sessions to help businesses understand the application process and improve their proposals. This comprehensive support ensures that more businesses can benefit from the available incentives."

Conclusion

As the seminar concluded, the audience felt motivated by the opportunities presented through government grants and subsidies. The session had provided valuable insights into the available support, the impact of subsidies, and the application process, highlighting the government's commitment to fostering a conducive investment climate.

Chanda addressed the audience one last time, "Zambia's grants and subsidy programs are designed to support strategic sectors and drive economic growth. By understanding and leveraging these incentives, investors can significantly enhance the viability and profitability of their projects in Zambia, contributing to the nation's sustainable development."

With that, the audience applauded, inspired by the potential to access government support for their ventures. The discussions and connections made at the seminar promised to pave the way for new investments, partnerships, and advancements in Zambia's economic landscape, ensuring continued growth and prosperity for the nation.

Public-Private Partnerships (PPPs)

The Zambia Public-Private Partnership Forum was a high-profile event attended by government officials, business leaders, and international investors at Mulungushi International Conference Center. The main hall was filled with the hum of discussions about the transformative potential of PPPs in Zambia's development. Chanda Mwamba, an expert in PPPs, prepared to share her knowledge on this critical topic.

"Good afternoon, esteemed guests," Chanda began, her voice

commanding attention. "Today, we will explore the Public-Private Partnership framework in Zambia, highlight some successful PPP projects, and discuss the opportunities and benefits for investors. Let's delve into how PPPs are shaping Zambia's infrastructure and economic landscape."

Overview of PPP Framework

Thandiwe Zulu, a senior advisor from the Ministry of Finance, took the floor. "Public-Private Partnerships are collaborative arrangements between the government and private sector entities to finance, develop, and operate infrastructure projects. The Zambian government has established a comprehensive PPP framework to facilitate these collaborations."

Chanda added, "The PPP framework in Zambia is governed by the Public-Private Partnership Act, which outlines the legal and regulatory environment for these projects. The Act provides guidelines on project identification, procurement, and implementation, ensuring transparency and accountability."

Mutinta Mwiinga, an infrastructure development consultant, elaborated, "The PPP framework aims to leverage private sector expertise, innovation, and capital to deliver public infrastructure projects more efficiently. This approach addresses funding gaps and accelerates the development of critical infrastructure."

Successful PPP Projects in Zambia

Kalenga Mukuka, an investment analyst, spoke next. "Zambia has witnessed several successful PPP projects that have had a significant impact on the country's development. These projects span various sectors, including transportation, energy, and healthcare."

Thandiwe Zulu highlighted, "One notable example is the Lusaka–Ndola Dual Carriageway project, a major infrastructure initiative aimed at improving road connectivity and reducing travel time between two of Zambia's key economic hubs. This project, implemented through a PPP arrangement, has enhanced trade and mobility."

Chanda nodded, "Another success story is the solar power project in Ngonye. Developed as a PPP, this project has increased Zambia's renewable energy capacity and contributed to the country's energy security. The involvement of private investors brought in technical expertise and capital, ensuring the project's success."

Mutinta added passionately, "The healthcare sector has also benefited from PPPs. The construction and operation of the Levy Mwanawasa Medical University was achieved through a PPP, providing world-class medical training and healthcare services. This project has improved healthcare access and capacity in Zambia."

Opportunities and Benefits for Investors

Wamundila Chikumbi, a senior representative from the Zambia Development Agency (ZDA), took the stage. "PPPs present numerous opportunities for investors across various sectors.

These partnerships allow investors to participate in large-scale infrastructure projects with government support, reducing risks and enhancing returns."

Mutinta Mwiinga elaborated, "Investors benefit from the stable regulatory environment, government guarantees, and access to long-term contracts. The collaborative nature of PPPs also means that investors can leverage government resources and networks to achieve project success."

Chanda highlighted, "Specific opportunities include infrastructure projects in transportation, such as road, rail, and airport developments; energy projects focusing on renewable sources; and social infrastructure projects in healthcare and education. The ZDA actively promotes these opportunities to attract investment."

Kalenga Mukuka emphasized, "The benefits for investors extend beyond financial returns. PPPs offer the chance to contribute to Zambia's sustainable development, enhance the quality of life for its citizens, and build a lasting legacy. These projects can significantly impact the country's economic and social landscape."

Conclusion

As the forum concluded, the audience felt invigorated by the potential of Public-Private Partnerships in Zambia. The session had provided valuable insights into the PPP framework, successful projects, and the opportunities and benefits for investors, highlighting the government's commitment to fostering these collaborative initiatives.

Chanda addressed the audience one last time, "Public-Private Partnerships are a powerful tool for driving infrastructure development and economic growth in Zambia. By understanding and engaging in PPPs, investors can play a pivotal role in shaping the future of our nation while reaping substantial rewards."

With that, the audience applauded, inspired by the transformative potential of PPPs. The discussions and connections made at the forum promised to pave the way for new investments, partnerships, and advancements in Zambia's infrastructure and economic landscape, ensuring continued growth and prosperity for the nation.

Export Incentives and Support

The Export Promotion Conference, a key event for businesses looking to expand into international markets, was in full swing at the Mulungushi International Conference Center in Lusaka. The hall was packed with entrepreneurs, export managers, and government officials eager to discuss the latest export incentives and support mechanisms. Chanda Mwamba, an expert in international trade, stood ready to guide the attendees through this crucial topic.

"Good afternoon, everyone," Chanda began, her voice filled with enthusiasm. "Today, we will explore the government support available for export-oriented businesses, the various export incentives and duty drawbacks, and the role of trade promotion agencies. Let's understand how these measures can help your businesses succeed in the global market."

Government Support for Export-Oriented Businesses

Thandiwe Zulu, a senior official from the Ministry of Commerce, Trade, and Industry, took the floor. "The Zambian government is committed to supporting businesses that aim to expand their operations beyond our borders. Various programs and initiatives have been put in place to assist export-oriented businesses."

Chanda added, "Government support includes access to finance, training, and capacity-building programs. The Zambia Development Agency (ZDA) offers grants and loans to help businesses improve their production capacities and meet international standards."

Mutinta Mwiinga, an export consultant, elaborated, "Additionally, the government provides technical assistance in market research and development. This helps businesses identify and understand potential markets, ensuring they are well-prepared to enter and compete in the global arena."

Export Incentives and Duty Drawbacks

Kalenga Mukuka, an international trade analyst, spoke next. "Export incentives are designed to make Zambian products more competitive in international markets. These incentives include tax breaks, subsidies, and duty drawbacks."

Thandiwe Zulu highlighted, "One of the key incentives is the duty drawback scheme, which allows exporters to claim a refund on import duties paid on raw materials and components used in the production of export goods. This reduces production costs and enhances the competitiveness of Zambian products."

Chanda nodded, "Tax incentives include exemptions and reductions on corporate income tax for export-oriented businesses. These incentives are particularly beneficial for manufacturers and agricultural producers, helping them increase their profit margins and reinvest in their operations."

Mutinta added passionately, "Export subsidies are also available to offset the costs associated with transportation and logistics. This support ensures that Zambian products can reach international markets at competitive prices, boosting export volumes and revenue."

Role of Trade Promotion Agencies

Wamundila Chikumbi, a senior representative from the Zambia Development Agency (ZDA), took the stage. "Trade promotion agencies like the ZDA play a crucial role in facilitating exports. Our mandate is to promote Zambian products in international markets and provide support to businesses throughout the export process."

Mutinta Mwiinga elaborated, "The ZDA organizes trade missions, exhibitions, and fairs to showcase Zambian products to potential buyers and investors. These events provide valuable networking opportunities and help businesses establish contacts with international partners."

Chanda highlighted, "The ZDA also offers export advisory services, assisting businesses with compliance to international standards and regulations. This ensures that Zambian products meet the quality requirements of target markets, enhancing their acceptability and competitiveness."

Kalenga Mukuka emphasized, "Furthermore, the ZDA collaborates with international trade organizations and bilateral chambers of commerce to promote Zambian exports. By leveraging these networks, the ZDA helps businesses access new markets and expand their global footprint."

Conclusion

As the conference concluded, the audience felt inspired by the comprehensive support and incentives available to export-oriented businesses in Zambia. The session had provided valuable insights into government support, export incentives, and the role of trade promotion agencies, highlighting the government's commitment to fostering a thriving export sector.

Chanda addressed the audience one last time, "Zambia's export incentives and support mechanisms are designed to help businesses succeed in the global market. By understanding and leveraging these measures, you can enhance your competitiveness and contribute to the growth and diversification of our economy."

With that, the audience applauded, inspired by the potential to access government support for their export ventures. The discussions and connections made at the conference promised to pave the way for new investments, partnerships, and advancements in Zambia's export landscape, ensuring continued growth and prosperity for the nation.

5

Chapter 5: Setting Up a Business in Zambia

Business Registration Procedures

The bustling lobby of the Zambia Development Agency (ZDA) headquarters was filled with aspiring entrepreneurs and business representatives seeking to navigate the complexities of setting up their ventures. Chanda Mwamba, a seasoned business consultant, was preparing to conduct a workshop on the business registration process. Among the attendees were Mutinta Mwiinga, an agribusiness entrepreneur, and Wamundila Chikumbi, a tech startup founder, both eager to learn the necessary steps to formalize their businesses.

"Welcome, everyone," Chanda began, her voice clear and reassuring. "Today, we're going to walk through the step-by-step process of registering a business in Zambia, identify the key government agencies involved, and discuss the timeframes and costs you should expect. Let's make sure you're fully equipped to start your business journey."

Step-by-Step Guide to Business Registration

Thandiwe Zulu, a senior official from the Patents and Companies Registration Agency (PACRA), took the floor. "The first step in registering your business is to choose and reserve a unique company name. This can be done online through the PACRA website or in person at any PACRA office."

Mutinta raised her hand, "How long does the name reservation take?"

Thandiwe smiled, "Typically, the name reservation process takes about 24 to 48 hours. Once your company name is approved, you'll receive a name reservation certificate, which is valid for 30 days."

Chanda continued, "Next, you'll need to prepare the necessary documents, including the Articles of Association and the company's bylaws. These documents outline the company's structure, objectives, and the responsibilities of directors and shareholders."

Wamundila asked, "What happens after we prepare these documents?"

Chanda replied, "You will submit these documents, along with the completed application forms, to PACRA. This can also be done online or in person. PACRA will review your application and, if everything is in order, they will issue a Certificate of Incorporation. This process usually takes about 3 to 5 business days."

Key Government Agencies Involved

Thandiwe Zulu elaborated, "Several key government agencies are involved in the business registration process. Besides PACRA, you will need to engage with the Zambia Revenue Authority (ZRA) to obtain a Taxpayer Identification Number (TPIN) and register for Value Added Tax (VAT) if applicable."

Chanda added, "You may also need to register with the National Pension Scheme Authority (NAPSA) for social security contributions and the Workers' Compensation Fund Control Board (WCFCB) if you have employees. These registrations ensure compliance with employment laws and social security regulations."

Mutinta looked thoughtful, "Are there any other agencies we should be aware of?"

Wamundila interjected, "Depending on your business type, you might also need licenses from sector-specific regulatory bodies. For example, if you're in the food industry, you'll need approval from the Zambia Bureau of Standards (ZABS) and the Zambia Environmental Management Agency (ZEMA)."

Timeframes and Costs

Kalenga Mukuka, a financial analyst, spoke next. "The timeframes and costs associated with business registration can vary. As mentioned, reserving a company name takes about 24 to 48 hours, and obtaining the Certificate of Incorporation takes 3 to 5 business days. Registering for taxes and social security can take an additional 1 to 2 weeks."

Chanda nodded, "In terms of costs, the name reservation fee is around ZMW 83 (USD 5), and the registration fee for a limited company is approximately ZMW 500 (USD 30). Additional costs may include legal fees for document preparation and sector-specific licenses."

Mutinta raised her hand again, "What if we need assistance throughout this process?"

Thandiwe responded, "PACRA, the ZDA, and other relevant agencies provide support services to help you navigate the registration process. There are also business consultants and legal firms specializing in company registration who can offer assistance, though their services come at an additional cost."

Conclusion

As the workshop concluded, the attendees felt empowered by the detailed guidance on the business registration process. Chanda had demystified the steps, highlighted the key agencies involved, and provided clear information on the timeframes and costs, making the journey to setting up a business in Zambia more approachable.

Chanda addressed the audience one last time, "Setting up a business in Zambia is a structured process that involves several steps and key agencies. By following the guidelines and leveraging available support, you can successfully register your business and embark on your entrepreneurial journey. Remember, thorough preparation and understanding of the requirements will pave the way for a smooth registration process."

With that, the audience applauded, inspired and ready to take the necessary steps to formalize their business ventures. The connections and knowledge gained at the workshop promised to pave the way for new businesses, partnerships, and contributions to Zambia's growing economy.

Legal and Regulatory Framework

The legal compliance workshop at the Zambia Development Agency headquarters was filled with entrepreneurs eager to understand the legal and regulatory landscape of setting up a business in Zambia. Chanda Mwamba, an expert in business law, prepared to guide the attendees through the critical aspects of legal compliance. Among the attendees were Mutinta Mwiinga, an agribusiness entrepreneur, and Wamundila Chikumbi, a tech startup founder, both keen to ensure their ventures adhered to Zambian laws.

"Good afternoon, everyone," Chanda began, her tone authoritative yet approachable. "Today, we will cover the legal and regulatory framework for setting up a business in Zambia. We'll provide an overview of business laws and regulations, discuss key compliance requirements, and delve into the protection of intellectual property rights. Let's ensure you have the knowledge to operate within the law and protect your interests."

Overview of Business Laws and Regulations

Thandiwe Zulu, a senior legal advisor from the Ministry of Justice, took the floor. "Zambia's business environment is governed by a comprehensive set of laws and regulations designed to promote fair practices and protect both businesses and consumers. The Companies Act, 2017, is the primary legislation regulating company formation, management, and dissolution."

Chanda added, "The Companies Act covers various aspects, including the incorporation process, duties of directors, shareholder rights, and financial reporting requirements. It ensures transparency and accountability in business operations."

Mutinta raised her hand, "What other laws should we be aware of?"

Thandiwe smiled, "Apart from the Companies Act, there are other important laws such as the Competition and Consumer Protection Act, the Employment Code Act, and the Income Tax Act. These laws regulate competition, labor relations, and taxation, respectively."

Chanda continued, "The Competition and Consumer Protection Act prevents anti-competitive practices and protects consumer rights, while the Employment Code Act governs employment contracts, working conditions, and employee rights. The Income Tax Act outlines the tax obligations of businesses, including corporate income tax, VAT, and other levies."

Key Compliance Requirements

Kalenga Mukuka, a compliance officer from the Zambia Revenue Authority (ZRA), spoke next. "Compliance is critical to operating legally in Zambia. Key compliance requirements include tax registration, filing annual returns, and adhering to labor laws."

Wamundila asked, "What are the specific tax compliance requirements?"

Kalenga replied, "Businesses must register for a Taxpayer Identification Number (TPIN) and, if applicable, for Value Added Tax (VAT). You are required to file annual tax returns and make quarterly provisional tax payments. Ensuring timely and accurate tax filing is essential to avoid penalties."

Mutinta inquired, "What about labor law compliance?"

Thandiwe Zulu responded, "Under the Employment Code Act, businesses must provide written employment contracts, adhere to minimum wage standards, and ensure safe working conditions. Additionally, employers must register with the National Pension Scheme Authority (NAPSA) for social security contributions and comply with the Workers' Compensation Fund Control Board (WCFCB) requirements."

Chanda emphasized, "It's also crucial to maintain proper financial records and submit annual financial statements to PACRA. Regular audits may be required depending on your business size and sector. Compliance with environmental regulations, particularly for industries like mining and agriculture, is also vital."

Intellectual Property Rights Protection

Mutinta Mwiinga, a business owner with a keen interest in protecting her brand, leaned forward as Chanda introduced the topic of intellectual property (IP) rights. "Protecting your intellectual property is essential to safeguarding your innovations, brands, and creations. Zambia has robust laws to protect IP rights."

Thandiwe elaborated, "The Patents Act, the Trademarks Act, and the Copyright and Performance Rights Act are the primary legislation governing IP in Zambia. These laws provide for the registration and protection of patents, trademarks, and copyrights."

Chanda added, "Registering your trademarks and patents

with PACRA ensures legal recognition and protection. This prevents unauthorized use of your intellectual property and allows you to take legal action against infringements."

Kalenga highlighted, "Copyright protection is automatic upon creation, but registration provides additional proof of ownership. It's crucial for businesses in the creative industries, such as software development, music, and literature, to understand and utilize these protections."

Conclusion

As the workshop concluded, the attendees felt empowered by the detailed guidance on the legal and regulatory framework for setting up a business in Zambia. Chanda had demystified the complexities, highlighted key compliance requirements, and emphasized the importance of protecting intellectual property.

Chanda addressed the audience one last time, "Understanding and adhering to the legal and regulatory framework is essential for the success and sustainability of your business. By ensuring compliance and protecting your intellectual property, you can operate confidently and focus on growing your venture."

With that, the audience applauded, inspired and ready to navigate the legal landscape. The connections and knowledge gained at the workshop promised to pave the way for new businesses, partnerships, and contributions to Zambia's growing economy.

Access to Finance and Banking Services

The Financial Access Symposium at the Bank of Zambia's grand hall was abuzz with activity. Entrepreneurs, bankers, and financial experts had gathered to discuss the crucial topic of accessing finance and banking services for businesses in Zambia. Chanda Mwamba, an experienced business consultant, was set to moderate the panel discussion. Among the attendees were Mutinta Mwiinga, an agribusiness entrepreneur, and Wamundila Chikumbi, a tech startup founder, both keen to explore their financing options.

"Good morning, everyone," Chanda began, her voice steady and confident. "Today, we will delve into the landscape of financial institutions in Zambia, explore various financing options for businesses, and understand the role of microfinance and development banks in supporting entrepreneurs. Let's equip you with the knowledge to secure the funding your business needs."

Overview of Financial Institutions

Thandiwe Zulu, a senior official from the Bank of Zambia, took the stage. "Zambia has a diverse range of financial institutions catering to different needs of businesses. These include commercial banks, microfinance institutions, and development banks."

Chanda added, "Commercial banks such as Zanaco, Stanbic Bank, and Barclays Bank offer a wide array of financial services including business loans, overdraft facilities, and trade finance. These banks are key players in providing capital to established businesses."

Mutinta raised her hand, "What about newer businesses or startups? Do they have the same access to these services?"

Thandiwe replied, "While commercial banks primarily serve established businesses, newer businesses can also access funding through microfinance institutions and development banks, which often have more flexible lending criteria."

Financing Options for Businesses

Kalenga Mukuka, a financial analyst, spoke next. "There are several financing options available for businesses in Zambia. These include traditional bank loans, equity financing, and grants."

Wamundila asked, "Can you explain the differences between these options?"

Kalenga nodded, "Bank loans are a common financing option where businesses borrow money from a bank and repay it with interest. Equity financing involves raising capital by selling shares of the company to investors. Grants, on the other hand, are funds provided by government or non-governmental organizations that do not need to be repaid."

Mutinta inquired, "How do businesses qualify for these loans?"

Chanda replied, "Qualification for bank loans typically requires a solid business plan, financial statements, and sometimes collateral. Equity financing might require you to pitch your business to investors, demonstrating its growth potential. Grants often have specific criteria and application processes, focusing on particular sectors or types of businesses."

Kalenga highlighted, "Development banks like the Development Bank of Zambia (DBZ) provide long-term financing for projects that contribute to economic development. They are particularly supportive of businesses in sectors such as agriculture, manufacturing, and infrastructure."

Role of Microfinance and Development Banks

Thandiwe Zulu returned to the discussion, "Microfinance institutions play a crucial role in providing financial services to small and medium-sized enterprises (SMEs) that might not qualify for traditional bank loans. These institutions offer smaller loan amounts with more flexible terms."

Chanda added, "Microfinance institutions like FINCA Zambia and Madison Finance provide microloans, savings accounts, and insurance products tailored to the needs of SMEs and entrepreneurs in underserved areas."

Mutinta asked, "How do development banks differ from microfinance institutions?"

Kalenga explained, "Development banks, such as the DBZ, focus on financing projects that have a significant impact on economic development. They offer larger loans with longer repayment periods compared to microfinance institutions. Their aim is to support projects that drive growth, create jobs, and improve infrastructure."

Wamundila leaned forward, "What specific initiatives do development banks support?"

Thandiwe responded, "Development banks support initiatives in sectors like agriculture, renewable energy, and industrial development. They often collaborate with international development agencies to provide funding and technical assistance for large-scale projects."

Conclusion

As the symposium concluded, the attendees felt empowered by the comprehensive insights into accessing finance and banking services. Chanda had provided a detailed overview of financial institutions, highlighted various financing options, and emphasized the critical role of microfinance and development banks.

Chanda addressed the audience one last time, "Accessing finance is a crucial step in setting up and growing your business. By understanding the landscape of financial institutions and the various financing options available, you can make informed decisions to secure the funding your business needs. Remember, whether through commercial banks, microfinance institutions, or development banks, there are resources available to support your entrepreneurial journey."

With that, the audience applauded, inspired and ready to explore their financing options. The connections and knowledge gained at the symposium promised to pave the way for new businesses, partnerships, and contributions to Zambia's growing economy.

Business Structures and Types

The Lusaka Innovation Hub was buzzing with the excitement of entrepreneurs ready to launch their ventures. Chanda Mwamba, an experienced business consultant, was preparing to guide the attendees through the different types of business structures available in Zambia. Among the eager participants were Mutinta Mwiinga, an agribusiness entrepreneur, and Wamundila Chikumbi, a tech startup founder.

"Good afternoon, everyone," Chanda began, her voice filled with enthusiasm. "Today, we will discuss the various business structures you can choose from when setting up your business in Zambia. We'll explore the types of business entities, the advantages and disadvantages of each structure, and how to choose the right one for your venture."

Types of Business Entities

Thandiwe Zulu, a legal advisor from the Ministry of Commerce, Trade, and Industry, took the stage. "Zambia offers several types of business entities, including sole proprietorships, partnerships, private limited companies, public limited companies, and cooperatives."

Chanda added, "A sole proprietorship is the simplest form, where one individual owns and operates the business. It's easy to set up and involves minimal regulatory requirements."

Mutinta raised her hand, "What about partnerships?"

Thandiwe replied, "Partnerships involve two or more individuals sharing ownership. There are general partnerships, where partners share equal responsibility and liability, and limited partnerships, where some partners have limited liability based on their investment."

Wamundila asked, "Can you explain the difference between private and public limited companies?"

Chanda explained, "A private limited company (Ltd) is owned by a small group of shareholders and does not trade its shares publicly. It offers limited liability protection and is suitable for small to medium-sized businesses. A public limited company (PLC), on the other hand, can sell shares to the public and is subject to stricter regulatory requirements. It's ideal for larger businesses looking to raise capital through the stock market."

Advantages and Disadvantages of Each Structure

Kalenga Mukuka, a financial analyst, spoke next. "Each business structure has its advantages and disadvantages. Sole proprietorships are easy and inexpensive to set up but come with unlimited personal liability."

Mutinta asked, "What about partnerships?"

Thandiwe responded, "Partnerships benefit from shared responsibility and combined skills, but partners are jointly liable for debts and obligations. In limited partnerships, liability is restricted to the amount invested by limited partners."

Chanda added, "Private limited companies offer limited liability protection, meaning shareholders' personal assets are protected. However, they involve more complex setup processes and regulatory compliance. Public limited companies can raise significant capital by selling shares, but they are subject to rigorous reporting requirements and greater public scrutiny."

Kalenga highlighted, "Cooperatives are another option, particularly for businesses focused on community or member benefits. They are democratically controlled by their members, who share profits and decision-making. However, cooperatives can be complex to manage and require active member participation."

Choosing the Right Business Structure

Thandiwe Zulu addressed the audience, "Choosing the right business structure depends on several factors, including the size and nature of your business, your liability preferences, tax considerations, and your long-term goals."

Mutinta looked thoughtful, "How do we decide which structure is best for us?"

Chanda replied, "Start by evaluating your business goals. If you're starting small and want full control, a sole proprietorship might be ideal. If you plan to collaborate with others and share responsibilities, consider a partnership. For limited liability and potential for growth, a private limited company could be the best choice. If you aim to raise capital from the public, a public limited company is suitable."

Kalenga added, "Consider the regulatory requirements and costs associated with each structure. Private and public limited companies require more compliance and reporting, which can be time-consuming and costly. Evaluate your ability to meet these obligations."

Wamundila asked, "What about tax implications?"

Thandiwe responded, "Tax implications vary by structure. Sole proprietorships and partnerships are taxed on personal income, while limited companies are subject to corporate tax rates. Cooperatives may benefit from tax exemptions or reductions based on their activities."

Conclusion

As the workshop concluded, the attendees felt empowered by the comprehensive insights into business structures and types. Chanda had provided a detailed overview of each structure, highlighted their advantages and disadvantages, and offered guidance on choosing the right one.

Chanda addressed the audience one last time, "Selecting the appropriate business structure is a critical decision that will impact your operations, liability, and growth potential. By understanding the characteristics of each entity and aligning them with your business goals, you can make an informed choice that sets you up for success."

With that, the audience applauded, inspired and ready to decide on the best business structure for their ventures. The connections and knowledge gained at the workshop promised to pave the way for new businesses, partnerships, and contributions to Zambia's growing economy.

Permits and Licensing

The Lusaka Business Expo was in full swing, attracting a diverse group of entrepreneurs eager to learn about the practicalities of setting up their businesses. One of the most anticipated sessions was the seminar on permits and licensing, led by Chanda Mwamba, a well-respected business consultant. Among the eager attendees were Mutinta Mwiinga, an agribusiness entrepreneur, and Wamundila Chikumbi, a tech startup founder.

"Good afternoon, everyone," Chanda began, her voice resonating through the conference room. "Today, we will discuss the permits and licenses necessary for setting up a business in Zambia. We'll provide an overview of the essential permits and licenses, the application process and requirements, and sector-specific licensing requirements. Understanding these elements is crucial to ensure your business operates legally and smoothly."

Overview of Necessary Permits and Licenses

Thandiwe Zulu, an official from the Patents and Companies Registration Agency (PACRA), took the stage. "In Zambia, most businesses need to obtain specific permits and licenses to operate legally. These vary depending on the type and location of your business."

Chanda added, "General permits include the business registration certificate from PACRA, a tax identification number (TPIN) from the Zambia Revenue Authority (ZRA), and possibly a trade license from the local municipal council."

Mutinta raised her hand, "Are there any other general licenses we should be aware of?"

Thandiwe replied, "Yes, depending on your business activities, you might need additional licenses such as health and safety permits from the Ministry of Health, especially if you are in the food and beverage industry, and environmental permits from the Zambia Environmental Management Agency (ZEMA) if your operations impact the environment."

Application Process and Requirements

Kalenga Mukuka, a compliance officer, spoke next. "The application process for permits and licenses involves several steps. First, ensure your business is registered with PACRA. This registration provides your business with legal recognition and is a prerequisite for most other permits."

Wamundila asked, "What are the typical requirements for these applications?"

Kalenga explained, "For most permits, you'll need to submit a completed application form, your PACRA registration certificate, a detailed business plan, and proof of address. Specific requirements vary by permit. For example, obtaining a TPIN from ZRA requires identification documents and proof of business registration."

Chanda highlighted, "It's essential to keep all your documentation organized and readily accessible. This will streamline the application process and help you avoid delays."

Mutinta inquired, "How long does it typically take to get these permits?"

Thandiwe responded, "The timeline varies depending on the type of permit and the efficiency of the issuing authority. Business registration with PACRA usually takes a few days to a week, while obtaining a trade license or environmental permit might take longer, often several weeks to a few months."

Sector-Specific Licensing Requirements

Thandiwe Zulu returned to the discussion, "Certain sectors have specific licensing requirements. For example, if you are in the agribusiness sector, you may need permits from the

Ministry of Agriculture, such as a phytosanitary certificate for exporting agricultural products."

Chanda added, "Similarly, businesses in the mining sector must obtain licenses from the Ministry of Mines and Mineral Development, including prospecting licenses, mining licenses, and mineral export permits. Each of these licenses has its own set of requirements and application procedures."

Wamundila asked, "What about the tech sector? Are there specific licenses we need?"

Kalenga replied, "For tech startups, you might need licenses from the Zambia Information and Communications Technology Authority (ZICTA). These include licenses for operating internet services, broadcasting, and other telecommunications services. Additionally, if you handle personal data, you must comply with data protection regulations."

Mutinta asked, "Are there any common challenges businesses face when applying for these permits?"

Thandiwe responded, "Common challenges include incomplete applications, delays in processing, and changes in regulatory requirements. It's crucial to stay informed about the latest regulations and ensure your applications are thorough and accurate."

Chanda emphasized, "Networking with other entrepreneurs and joining business associations can provide valuable insights and support during the application process. These connections can help you navigate any challenges that arise."

Conclusion

As the seminar concluded, the attendees felt more confident about navigating the complex landscape of permits and licenses required for setting up a business in Zambia. Chanda had provided a clear overview, detailed the application process, and highlighted sector-specific requirements.

Chanda addressed the audience one last time, "Securing the necessary permits and licenses is a vital step in ensuring your business operates legally and efficiently. By understanding the requirements and staying organized, you can navigate this process successfully. Remember, thorough preparation and staying informed are key to avoiding delays and complications."

With that, the audience applauded, inspired and ready to tackle the licensing requirements for their ventures. The connections and knowledge gained at the seminar promised to pave the way for new businesses, partnerships, and contributions to Zambia's growing economy.

6

Chapter 6: Labor Market and Human Resources

Labor Laws and Regulations

The spacious conference room was filled with HR managers, business owners, and legal advisors attending a corporate training workshop on labor laws and regulations in Zambia. Among the attendees were Nchimunya Banda, an HR manager at a multinational company; Misozi Mwale, an entrepreneur looking to expand her business; and Chilufya Tembo, a labor law consultant.

Overview of Labor Laws in Zambia

The session began with Chilufya Tembo taking the stage. "Good morning, everyone. Today, we will delve into the labor laws that govern employment in Zambia," he said, addressing the audience. "Understanding these laws is crucial for fostering a compliant and fair workplace."

He continued, "The Employment Act is the cornerstone of labor legislation in Zambia. It outlines the basic conditions of employment, including minimum wage, working hours, overtime, leave entitlements, and termination procedures. Additionally, the Industrial and Labour Relations Act addresses the rights of workers to form and join trade unions, as well as the mechanisms for resolving industrial disputes."

Nchimunya raised her hand, "How do these laws impact our day-to-day HR practices?"

Chilufya responded, "They provide a framework for ensuring that employment contracts are fair and transparent, protecting both employers and employees. Adhering to these laws not only minimizes legal risks but also promotes a positive work environment."

Key Regulations for Employers

Next, the focus shifted to key regulations for employers. "Employers have several obligations under Zambian labor laws," Chilufya explained. "These include providing safe working conditions, paying salaries on time, ensuring that working hours do not exceed legal limits, and granting leave entitlements such as annual leave, sick leave, and maternity leave."

He added, "Employers must also comply with statutory deductions such as the National Pension Scheme Authority (NAPSA) contributions and pay-as-you-earn (PAYE) tax. Regular training and awareness programs for both management and staff are essential to maintain compliance and foster a culture of respect and fairness."

Rights and Obligations of Employees

Chilufya then addressed the rights and obligations of employees. "Employees in Zambia have the right to fair remuneration, safe working conditions, and the ability to join trade unions. They are entitled to protection from unfair dismissal and discrimination based on race, gender, religion, or disability."

Misozi Mwale, curious about employee responsibilities, asked, "What obligations do employees have towards their employers?"

"Employees are expected to perform their duties with diligence and integrity," Chilufya replied. "They must adhere to company policies, respect working hours, and maintain confidentiality regarding sensitive business information. In essence, a balanced approach where both parties fulfill their obligations is key to a harmonious employment relationship."

Conclusion

As the workshop concluded, participants engaged in discussions about implementing best practices in their organizations. Nchimunya and Misozi exchanged ideas on enhancing employee engagement and compliance with labor laws, inspired by the comprehensive overview provided by Chilufya.

Chilufya's final words resonated with the attendees: "Navigating the complexities of labor laws and regulations is vital for any successful business. By understanding and implementing these laws effectively, we create workplaces that are not only legally compliant but also conducive to growth and productivity for both employers and employees."

With newfound knowledge and a commitment to fostering

fair employment practices, Nchimunya, Misozi, and the other participants left the workshop ready to implement positive changes within their organizations, contributing to a more just and productive labor market in Zambia.

Skillset and Availability of Workforce

The National Workforce Development Conference in Lusaka was a highly anticipated event, drawing policymakers, industry leaders, and educators from across Zambia. The conference hall was abuzz with discussions on enhancing the skillset and availability of the workforce to meet the country's growing economic demands. Among the attendees were Thandiwe Phiri, a government official focused on education and training; Mwamba Musonda, an executive from a leading manufacturing company; and Sipho Ndlovu, a representative from a private vocational training institute.

Overview of Labor Market and Workforce Skills

Thandiwe Phiri began the session with an overview of Zambia's labor market. "Ladies and gentlemen, thank you for being here today. As we know, Zambia's labor market is dynamic and evolving, with a young and growing population that presents both opportunities and challenges," she said. "Our workforce is characterized by a diverse range of skills, but there is a significant need to align these skills with market demands."

She highlighted data from recent labor market surveys, showing areas of strength and gaps in workforce skills. "While we have a strong base of agricultural workers and a growing number of professionals in sectors like finance and IT, there is a critical need for technical and vocational skills, particularly in the manufacturing and mining industries."

Key Sectors and Skill Demand

Mwamba Musonda then took the podium to discuss the key sectors and their skill demands. "In the manufacturing sector, we are seeing rapid growth, but this growth is hindered by a shortage of skilled labor," he explained. "We need more technicians, engineers, and quality control specialists to keep up with the technological advancements and production needs."

He continued, "Similarly, the mining sector, which is a cornerstone of our economy, requires a steady influx of skilled workers. This includes geologists, mining engineers, and environmental scientists. The service sector is also expanding, especially in areas like tourism and hospitality, where skilled personnel are crucial for maintaining high standards."

Sipho Ndlovu nodded in agreement, preparing to discuss how his institute was addressing these demands.

Government and Private Sector Training Programs

Finally, Sipho Ndlovu addressed the audience. "To meet these demands, we need a concerted effort from both the government and the private sector in training and development," he stated. "Our institute, for example, offers specialized vocational training programs that equip students with practical skills tailored to industry needs."

He outlined various successful training programs and partnerships with businesses. "We've collaborated with manufacturing firms to provide hands-on training and internships, ensuring that graduates are job-ready. Additionally, government initiatives such as the Technical Education, Vocational and Entrepreneurship Training Authority (TEVETA) are crucial in standardizing and supporting these efforts."

Thandiwe added, "The government is also investing in education reforms and infrastructure to improve the quality of training. We are working towards creating a more robust system that not only addresses current skill gaps but also anticipates future needs."

Conclusion

As the session concluded, attendees engaged in animated discussions about the future of Zambia's workforce. Thandiwe, Mwamba, and Sipho exchanged ideas on how to further strengthen the collaboration between government and private sector to enhance workforce skills.

Thandiwe's closing remarks echoed the shared sentiment of the conference: "By aligning our training programs with market demands and fostering strong partnerships, we can build a workforce that drives Zambia's economic growth and development. Together, we can create opportunities for our young population and ensure that Zambia remains competitive on the global stage."

With a renewed sense of purpose and a commitment to fostering skill development, Thandiwe, Mwamba, Sipho, and the other participants left the conference inspired to implement strategies that would bridge the skill gaps and unlock the full potential of Zambia's workforce.

Establishing Compensation and Benefits Packages

The Lusaka Business Conference was abuzz with entrepreneurs and HR professionals gathering for an insightful seminar on establishing compensation and benefits packages. Chanda Mwamba, a seasoned HR consultant, stood at the front, ready to impart crucial knowledge. Among the attentive attendees were Mutinta Mwiinga, a passionate agribusiness owner, and Wamundila Chikumbi, a determined tech startup founder.

Competitive Salary Benchmarks

Chanda started with a commanding voice, "Welcome, everyone, to our discussion on compensation and benefits. Today, we'll explore the importance of competitive salary benchmarks, the perks and benefits that attract top talent, and effective strategies for retaining them."

Thandiwe Zulu, a respected economist, joined in, "In Zambia, it's essential to benchmark salaries against industry standards to ensure competitiveness and fairness. This practice not only attracts skilled professionals but also motivates existing employees."

Benefits and Perks for Employees

Kalenga Mukuka, a financial analyst, added, "Benefits and perks play a crucial role in employee satisfaction. Beyond salary, employees value health insurance, retirement plans, and bonuses. Non-monetary benefits such as flexible work hours and professional development opportunities also contribute significantly."

Mutinta raised her hand, "What are some innovative benefits that companies can offer?"

Chanda smiled, "Companies are increasingly offering wellness programs, gym memberships, and even childcare facilities. These perks enhance work-life balance and contribute to a positive work environment."

Strategies for Attracting and Retaining Talent

Wamundila, intrigued, asked, "How can startups with limited resources compete for top talent?"

Thandiwe responded, "Startups can differentiate themselves by offering equity ownership, which aligns employees' interests with the company's success. Additionally, showcasing a vibrant company culture and opportunities for career growth can attract ambitious professionals."

Chanda concluded, "Ultimately, establishing competitive compensation and benefits packages requires understanding your industry norms, listening to employee feedback, and continuously adapting to meet evolving expectations. By prioritizing employee well-being and career development, businesses can create a workplace where talent thrives and contributes to long-term success."

As the seminar wrapped up, attendees exchanged contacts and ideas, energized by the insights gained. Mutinta and Wamundila left with a clearer vision of how to structure their compensation and benefits packages to attract and retain the best talent for their growing businesses.

Health and Safety Regulations

In the heart of Lusaka's bustling industrial zone, a workshop on workplace health and safety regulations was underway. Chanda Mwamba, an experienced HR consultant, stood before a diverse group of business owners and managers. Among them were Mutinta Mwiinga, a dedicated agribusiness entrepreneur, and Wamundila Chikumbi, a tech startup founder eager to learn about ensuring safety in their workplace.

Overview of Workplace Health and Safety Laws

Chanda began, her voice commanding attention, "Good morning, everyone. Today, we're diving into workplace health and safety regulations in Zambia. It's crucial for every business to comply with these laws to protect employees' well-being and maintain productivity."

Thandiwe Zulu, a regulatory compliance expert, joined in, "Zambia's laws require businesses to provide a safe and healthy working environment for all employees. This includes measures to prevent accidents, injuries, and occupational diseases."

Key Compliance Requirements

Kalenga Mukuka, a safety officer, spoke next, "Compliance requirements include conducting risk assessments, implementing safety measures, providing appropriate training, and maintaining records of incidents and safety inspections."

Mutinta raised her hand, "What are some specific safety measures businesses should implement?"

Thandiwe responded, "Businesses should establish emergency procedures, provide personal protective equipment (PPE) where necessary, and ensure proper ventilation and sanitation. Regular inspections and maintenance of equipment and facilities are also essential."

Best Practices for Ensuring Workplace Safety

Wamundila, curious, asked, "What are some best practices to enhance workplace safety?"

Chanda smiled, "Effective communication and employee involvement are key. Encourage workers to report hazards and near-misses promptly. Training programs on safety protocols and emergency responses empower employees to act confidently in any situation."

Thandiwe added, "Promoting a safety culture where everyone takes responsibility for their own and others' well-being fosters a positive work environment. Regular safety meetings and updates ensure that safety remains a priority."

Conclusion

As the workshop concluded, attendees exchanged insights and committed to implementing robust health and safety measures in their workplaces. Mutinta and Wamundila left with a renewed commitment to prioritizing their employees' safety and well-being, knowing that a safe workplace is fundamental to their business's success and growth in Zambia's dynamic economy.

Talent Development and Employee Training

At the Zambia Business Academy, a seminar on talent development and employee training was in full swing. Chanda Mwamba, a seasoned HR consultant, stood before a group of enthusiastic business owners and managers. Among them were Mutinta Mwiinga, a passionate agribusiness entrepreneur, and Wamundila Chikumbi, a tech startup founder eager to enhance their workforce's skills.

Training and Development Programs

Chanda began, her voice resonating through the room, "Good afternoon, everyone. Today, we're exploring the importance of talent development and employee training. Investing in your employees' skills not only enhances productivity but also fosters loyalty and innovation within your organization."

Thandiwe Zulu, a training specialist, added, "Training programs should align with your business objectives and employees' career aspirations. They can range from technical skills training to leadership development and customer service excellence."

Government and Private Sector Initiatives

Kalenga Mukuka, an industry expert, spoke next, "Both the government and private sector play vital roles in supporting employee training initiatives. Government programs provide subsidies and grants to businesses investing in skills development. Private sector partnerships offer specialized training programs tailored to industry needs."

Mutinta raised her hand, "What are some examples of government initiatives?"

Thandiwe responded, "The Zambia Development Agency (ZDA) and Technical Education, Vocational and Entrepreneurship Training Authority (TEVETA) offer funding and accreditation for training programs. These initiatives aim to enhance workforce capabilities and drive economic growth."

Importance of Continuous Professional Development

Wamundila, intrigued, asked, "Why is continuous professional development important?"

Chanda smiled, "Continuous learning keeps employees engaged and adaptable in a rapidly changing business environment. It equips them with new skills and knowledge to tackle challenges and seize opportunities. By investing in their growth, businesses cultivate a motivated and skilled workforce."

Thandiwe added, "Professional development also strengthens your employer brand and attracts top talent. Employees value organizations that invest in their career progression and offer opportunities for continuous learning."

Conclusion

As the seminar concluded, attendees exchanged ideas and committed to implementing robust talent development strategies in their organizations. Mutinta and Wamundila left with a renewed focus on nurturing their employees' potential through structured training programs and continuous professional development initiatives. They understood that investing in their workforce not only drives business success but also contributes to Zambia's vibrant economic landscape.

7

Chapter 7: Land Acquisition and Property Rights

Types of Land Ownership in Zambia

In the heart of a rural village in Zambia, a community meeting was held under the large baobab tree that served as a gathering point for the villagers. Attendees included local farmers, community leaders, and representatives from the Ministry of Lands. Among them were Mwape Chanda, a respected village elder; Lombe Kunda, a young entrepreneur interested in acquiring land for an agribusiness project; and Nkandu Mwewa, a government official tasked with explaining land ownership policies.

Overview of Land Categories

Nkandu Mwewa stood in front of the gathered crowd, addressing the villagers with a warm smile. "Good afternoon, everyone. Thank you for coming. Today, we will discuss the different categories of land ownership in Zambia, which is crucial for anyone looking to acquire land, whether for personal or business purposes," she began.

She pulled out a large, detailed map of Zambia, pointing to various regions. "In Zambia, land is primarily classified into two categories: customary land and state land. Customary land is managed by traditional leaders and makes up about 94% of the land in Zambia. State land, on the other hand, is managed by the government and constitutes about 6% of the total land area."

Customary vs. Statutory Land Ownership

Mwape Chanda, with his deep knowledge of local traditions, added, "Customary land has been governed by our chiefs and headmen for generations. Land rights are typically passed down through families, and the community works together to resolve any disputes."

Nkandu nodded in agreement. "That's correct, Mr. Chanda. Customary land offers a sense of community and continuity, but it can be challenging to formalize ownership. On the other hand, statutory land ownership, which includes leasehold and freehold, provides more formal and legally recognized ownership. This type of land can be registered with the Ministry of Lands, providing clearer rights and easier access to credit and investments."

Lombe Kunda, eager to understand the practical implications, asked, "What are the main differences in terms of rights and restrictions for someone like me who wants to start a business on this land?"

CHAPTER 7: LAND ACQUISITION AND PROPERTY RIGHTS

Rights and Restrictions for Foreign Investors

Nkandu explained, "For Zambian citizens, acquiring both customary and statutory land is relatively straightforward. However, foreign investors face certain restrictions. Foreigners cannot own land outright; they can only lease land for up to 99 years. This lease must be approved by the President and is subject to specific conditions aimed at ensuring the land is used for productive purposes."

She continued, "For customary land, foreign investors must engage with local chiefs and obtain consent from the community. This often involves demonstrating how their project will benefit the local population, such as through job creation or community development projects."

Mwape added, "It's important for foreigners to respect our customs and traditions when negotiating for customary land. Building trust and understanding with the community is crucial for the success of any venture."

Nkandu emphasized, "Transparency and adherence to regulations are key. The Ministry of Lands provides guidelines and support to ensure that both local and foreign investors can navigate the process efficiently. It's also advisable to seek legal advice to understand all the legal obligations and protections available."

Conclusion

As the meeting drew to a close, the attendees felt a deeper understanding of the complexities of land ownership in Zambia. Mwape, Lombe, and the other villagers discussed how they could leverage this knowledge for community development and personal ventures.

Nkandu's final words resonated with the group: "Understanding the types of land ownership and the associated rights and restrictions is essential for making informed decisions about land acquisition. Whether you are a local farmer or a foreign investor, knowing the rules and building strong relationships with the community and authorities will pave the way for successful land use and development."

With this newfound knowledge, Lombe felt more confident about his agribusiness project, and the villagers were better equipped to manage their land resources effectively, ensuring that the benefits of development were shared by all.

Leasing and Acquisition Procedures

In a bustling government office in Lusaka, several individuals were gathered to navigate the process of acquiring land. Present were Lombe Kunda, the young entrepreneur from the rural village; Mrs. Mwansa, an experienced land officer; and Mr. Chisala, a representative from the Ministry of Lands.

Steps for Acquiring Land in Zambia

Lombe sat across from Mrs. Mwansa, eager to understand the steps involved in acquiring land for his agribusiness project. Mrs. Mwansa smiled reassuringly and began to explain, "Mr. Kunda, the process for acquiring land in Zambia involves several key steps. First, you need to identify the land you want to lease or buy. For customary land, this involves discussions with the local chief and community, as we discussed previously. For state land, you'll need to find a suitable plot that is available for lease."

Mr. Chisala, chiming in, added, "Once you've identified the land, you'll need to submit an application to the Ministry of Lands. This application includes detailed plans for how you intend to use the land, and it must be accompanied by various supporting documents, such as proof of identity, business registration documents, and a site plan."

Mrs. Mwansa continued, "After submitting your application, it undergoes a review process where we verify the details and ensure everything is in order. This may also involve an inspection of the land to confirm its suitability for your proposed use."

Key Government Agencies Involved

Lombe, jotting down notes, asked, "Which government agencies will I need to interact with during this process?"

Mr. Chisala replied, "Several key agencies are involved. The Ministry of Lands is the primary authority overseeing land transactions. For state land, you may also need to work with the Zambia Environmental Management Agency (ZEMA) if your project requires an environmental impact assessment. For business-related land use, you might also engage with the Zambia Development Agency (ZDA) to ensure your project aligns with national investment policies."

Mrs. Mwansa added, "If you're dealing with customary land, the local council and traditional authorities play a crucial role in granting initial consent before the Ministry of Lands can formalize the lease. Coordination with these entities is essential to streamline the process."

Costs and Timelines

Lombe looked up from his notes, "What about the costs and timelines involved?"

Mrs. Mwansa explained, "The costs can vary depending on the type and size of the land, as well as its location. There are application fees, survey fees, and lease fees that you'll need to budget for. Additionally, if your project requires environmental assessments, there may be extra costs associated with those."

Mr. Chisala elaborated, "Timelines can also vary. On average, the entire process for acquiring state land can take between six months to a year, depending on the complexity of the application and how quickly you can provide the necessary documentation. Customary land acquisition might be quicker in terms of initial agreements but could still take several months to formalize through the Ministry of Lands."

Conclusion

As the meeting concluded, Lombe felt more informed and prepared for the journey ahead. Mrs. Mwansa's clear explanations and Mr. Chisala's insights had provided him with a roadmap for navigating the land acquisition process.

Mrs. Mwansa's final advice was practical and encouraging, "Mr. Kunda, the key to a smooth acquisition process is thorough preparation and patience. Make sure you have all your documents ready and maintain clear communication with all the involved agencies. And remember, we're here to help you every step of the way."

With a determined smile, Lombe thanked them both, ready to

embark on the next phase of his agribusiness venture, confident that he had the knowledge and support needed to successfully acquire the land and bring his project to life.

Environmental Considerations

In a spacious conference room in Lusaka, an environmental workshop was underway, organized by the Zambia Environmental Management Agency (ZEMA). Attendees included government officials, environmental experts, and prospective investors like Lombe Kunda. Among the speakers were Ms. Chilufya, an environmental scientist, and Dr. Banda, a senior ZEMA official.

Environmental Regulations and Compliance

Ms. Chilufya stood at the podium, addressing the attendees. "Good morning, everyone. Today, we will discuss the critical aspect of environmental considerations in land acquisition and development projects. In Zambia, we have stringent environmental regulations to ensure that development is sustainable and does not harm our natural resources."

She continued, "All investors must comply with the Environmental Management Act. This legislation mandates that any significant land development project must adhere to environmental standards set by ZEMA. Compliance ensures that projects are not only legally sound but also environmentally responsible."

Dr. Banda added, "Non-compliance with these regulations can lead to severe penalties, including fines and project shutdowns. It's crucial for investors to understand and integrate these regulations from the outset to avoid any legal or operational issues."

Environmental Impact Assessments (EIAs)

Lombe, keen on understanding the specifics, raised his hand. "Could you explain the role of Environmental Impact Assessments in this process?"

Ms. Chilufya nodded. "Absolutely, Mr. Kunda. An Environmental Impact Assessment, or EIA, is a comprehensive study that evaluates the potential environmental effects of a proposed project. This assessment is essential for identifying and mitigating negative impacts on the environment."

Dr. Banda elaborated, "The EIA process involves several steps. First, you submit a project brief to ZEMA, outlining your proposed activities. Based on this brief, we determine the level of assessment required. If an EIA is necessary, you'll need to conduct detailed studies, often involving consultations with local communities and experts. The final EIA report must include mitigation measures for any identified environmental risks."

Lombe asked, "How long does the EIA process typically take?"

Dr. Banda replied, "The timeline for an EIA can vary, but it generally takes several months. It's a thorough process designed to ensure that all potential impacts are considered and addressed. Starting the EIA early in your project planning can help avoid delays later on."

Sustainable Land Use Practices

As the discussion progressed, the focus shifted to sustainable land use practices. Ms. Chilufya emphasized, "Sustainable land use is about balancing development needs with environmental protection. For example, in agricultural projects, using eco-friendly farming techniques can minimize soil degradation and water pollution."

She shared a case study, "One successful example is a project in the Eastern Province where investors implemented conservation agriculture techniques. These methods not only increased crop yields but also preserved the soil and reduced the need for chemical fertilizers."

Dr. Banda concluded, "Integrating sustainable practices into your projects is not just about compliance; it's about ensuring long-term viability. Projects that respect and protect the environment often gain greater community support and can attract additional funding from environmentally conscious investors."

Conclusion

As the workshop wrapped up, Lombe felt more equipped with the knowledge necessary to navigate the environmental aspects of his agribusiness project. The insights from Ms. Chilufya and Dr. Banda had highlighted the importance of environmental stewardship in successful land development.

Dr. Banda's parting words resonated with the attendees, "Remember, sustainable development is the key to a prosperous future. By adhering to environmental regulations and adopting sustainable practices, we can ensure that our projects benefit both the economy and the environment."

With a sense of responsibility and a clear understanding of the environmental considerations, Lombe left the workshop, ready to incorporate these vital elements into his project plans, ensuring his venture would be both profitable and environmentally sustainable.

Property Development and Zoning Laws

Amidst the vibrant atmosphere of the Lusaka Real Estate Summit, property developers and investors gathered for a forum on property development and zoning laws. Chanda Mwamba, a distinguished legal expert in real estate, stood at the forefront, ready to delve into the intricacies of property development in Zambia. Among the attentive audience were Mutinta Mwiinga, a determined agribusiness entrepreneur eyeing expansion, and Wamundila Chikumbi, a tech innovator exploring new office space options.

Overview of Property Development Laws

Chanda began, her voice projecting authority and knowledge, "Good morning, esteemed developers and investors. Today, we're navigating the landscape of property development laws in Zambia. These laws govern the planning, construction, and use of properties, ensuring sustainable urban development and environmental protection."

Thandiwe Zulu, a zoning specialist, added, "Understanding property development laws is crucial for compliance and successful project execution. These laws dictate the permissible land use, building standards, and environmental impact assessments required for development projects."

Zoning Regulations and Their Impact

Kalenga Mukuka, an urban planner, continued, "Zoning regulations designate areas for residential, commercial, industrial, and recreational use. They aim to manage urban growth, preserve natural resources, and ensure compatibility among neighboring properties."

Mutinta raised her hand, "How do zoning regulations impact property developers?"

Thandiwe explained, "Zoning determines the type of activities permissible in specific areas. For instance, residential zones may restrict commercial activities to maintain a quiet neighborhood environment. Developers must adhere to these regulations to obtain building permits and avoid legal complications."

Key Considerations for Property Developers

Wamundila, eager to learn, asked, "What are some key considerations for developers navigating these regulations?"

Chanda nodded, "Developers must conduct thorough feasibility studies, including environmental assessments and community impact evaluations. Engaging with local authorities and communities early in the planning phase fosters transparency and mitigates potential conflicts."

Thandiwe added, "Compliance with building codes, height restrictions, setback requirements, and infrastructure provisions is essential. Engaging legal and zoning experts ensures projects align with regulatory standards and enhances project viability."

Conclusion

As the forum concluded, developers exchanged insights and strategies for navigating property development laws and zoning regulations in Zambia. Mutinta and Wamundila left with a deeper understanding of the regulatory landscape, equipped to approach their upcoming projects with diligence and compliance. They recognized that adhering to property development laws not only ensures legal compliance but also contributes to sustainable urban growth and community development in Zambia.

Dispute Resolution and Legal Remedies

In the serene halls of the Lusaka Law Institute, a seminar on property disputes and legal remedies drew a diverse crowd of lawyers, investors, and concerned citizens. Chanda Mwamba, a seasoned property law expert, stood at the lectern, ready to dissect the complexities of dispute resolution in Zambia. Among the attendees were Mutinta Mwiinga, a determined agribusiness owner facing land tenure challenges, and Wamundila Chikumbi, a tech entrepreneur interested in understanding legal safeguards for property investments.

Common Land Disputes and Resolution Mechanisms

Chanda began, her voice authoritative yet approachable, "Good afternoon, esteemed guests. Today, we're delving into common land disputes and the mechanisms available for resolution.

Land tenure issues, boundary disputes, and ownership conflicts are prevalent in Zambia's diverse property landscape."

Thandiwe Zulu, a dispute resolution specialist, added, "Resolution mechanisms include negotiation, mediation, and arbitration. These approaches aim to resolve disputes amicably, preserving relationships and minimizing legal costs."

Role of Courts and Alternative Dispute Resolution

Kalenga Mukuka, a litigation expert, continued, "Courts play a pivotal role in adjudicating complex property disputes where legal principles and precedents guide decisions. Alternatively, alternative dispute resolution (ADR) methods like mediation and arbitration offer faster, more flexible resolutions outside the courtroom."

Mutinta raised her hand, "What are the advantages of ADR over traditional court litigation?"

Thandiwe explained, "ADR encourages parties to collaborate in reaching mutually acceptable solutions. It promotes confidentiality, preserves business relationships, and often results in quicker resolutions compared to lengthy court proceedings."

Legal Remedies Available to Investors

Wamundila, curious about safeguarding investments, asked, "What legal remedies are available to investors in case of property disputes?"

Chanda nodded, "Investors have access to various legal remedies, including specific performance orders to enforce contract terms, damages for financial losses due to breaches, and injunctions to halt unauthorized activities. Legal remedies ensure investors' rights are protected under Zambian law."

Conclusion

As the seminar concluded, attendees engaged in spirited discussions, exchanging insights and strategies for navigating property disputes in Zambia. Mutinta and Wamundila left with a deeper understanding of dispute resolution mechanisms and legal safeguards, prepared to safeguard their investments and navigate potential challenges in Zambia's dynamic property market. They recognized that proactive engagement with legal experts and adherence to dispute resolution principles are essential for successful property transactions and sustainable business growth.

8

Chapter 8: Sustainable Business Practices in Zambia

Corporate Social Responsibility (CSR) Initiatives

At the prestigious Lusaka Business Forum, a workshop on Corporate Social Responsibility (CSR) initiatives gathered a diverse group of business leaders, CSR professionals, and community advocates. Chanda Mwamba, a respected CSR consultant, stood before the attentive audience, including Mutinta Mwiinga, a dedicated agribusiness owner, and Wamundila Chikumbi, a tech entrepreneur committed to ethical business practices.

Overview of CSR in Zambia

Chanda began, her voice resonating with passion, "Good morning, esteemed guests. Today, we explore the essence of Corporate Social Responsibility in Zambia. CSR goes beyond profitability; it encompasses how businesses contribute positively to society through ethical practices and community engagement."

Thandiwe Zulu, an CSR expert, joined in, "In Zambia, CSR initiatives focus on sustainable development, environmental stewardship, education, healthcare, and community empowerment. These initiatives align business objectives with societal needs, fostering mutual benefits."

Key CSR Activities and Their Impact

Kalenga Mukuka, a sustainability advocate, added, "CSR activities include supporting education through scholarships and school infrastructure development, promoting environmental conservation through tree planting and waste management initiatives, and empowering communities through skills training and healthcare access."

Mutinta raised her hand, "What impact do these CSR activities have on businesses?"

Thandiwe explained, "CSR enhances corporate reputation and brand loyalty. Engaging with communities builds trust and goodwill, fostering long-term relationships with stakeholders. It also attracts socially conscious consumers and investors who value ethical business practices."

Benefits of CSR for Businesses

Wamundila, eager to learn, asked, "What are some specific benefits of CSR for businesses in Zambia?"

Chanda smiled, "CSR enhances employee morale and productivity by fostering a sense of purpose and pride in the organization. It mitigates risks by promoting ethical behavior and regulatory compliance. Moreover, it drives innovation and sustainable business practices, positioning companies for long-term success."

Thandiwe added, "By integrating CSR into business strategies, companies contribute to Zambia's socio-economic development, creating shared value for stakeholders and society at large."

Conclusion

As the workshop concluded, participants exchanged ideas and committed to integrating impactful CSR initiatives into their business models. Mutinta and Wamundila left inspired, understanding that CSR is not only a responsibility but also an opportunity to make a meaningful difference in Zambia's communities while fostering sustainable business growth. They were determined to implement robust CSR strategies that align with their business goals and contribute positively to Zambia's vibrant socio-economic fabric.

Building a Sustainable Supply Chain

Amidst the bustling Zambia Business Summit, a dedicated session on building sustainable supply chains attracted a diverse audience of industry leaders, sustainability experts, and entrepreneurs. Chanda Mwamba, a seasoned sustainability consultant, stood at the forefront, ready to explore the intricacies of sustainable sourcing and supply chain practices. Among the attendees were Mutinta Mwiinga, an ambitious agribusiness owner, and Wamundila Chikumbi, a tech innovator keen on integrating sustainability into his business operations.

Importance of Sustainability in Supply Chains

Chanda began, her voice commanding attention, "Good afternoon, esteemed guests. Today, we delve into the critical role of sustainability in supply chains. Sustainable practices not only mitigate environmental impact but also enhance operational efficiency, reduce costs, and foster resilience in a rapidly evolving market."

Thandiwe Zulu, a sustainability strategist, joined in, "In Zambia, businesses are increasingly adopting sustainable sourcing practices to meet consumer demand for ethical products. These practices encompass responsible sourcing of raw materials, reducing carbon footprint, and promoting fair labor practices across the supply chain."

Strategies for Sustainable Sourcing

Kalenga Mukuka, a supply chain expert, continued, "Strategies include partnering with suppliers committed to environmental stewardship and ethical labor practices. Conducting life cycle assessments to measure environmental impact, implementing traceability systems, and engaging in supplier audits ensure transparency and compliance with sustainability standards."

Mutinta raised her hand, "Could you provide examples of successful sustainable practices?"

Thandiwe shared enthusiastically, "Certainly! In the agricultural sector, companies are implementing organic farming methods, promoting biodiversity conservation, and using renewable energy in production processes. In manufacturing, initiatives focus on waste reduction, energy efficiency, and ethical sourcing of materials."

Case Studies of Successful Sustainable Practices

Wamundila, eager to learn from practical examples, asked, "Can you share any case studies of successful sustainable practices in Zambia?"

Chanda nodded, "Certainly. One notable example is a local textile company that reduced water consumption by implementing closed-loop water recycling systems. Another case involves a mining company that rehabilitated mining sites and invested in community-based reforestation projects, demonstrating commitment to environmental stewardship and community engagement."

Conclusion

As the conference concluded, participants engaged in lively discussions and networking, inspired to integrate sustainable practices into their supply chains. Mutinta and Wamundila left with actionable insights, motivated to adopt innovative strategies that align with their business values and contribute positively to Zambia's sustainable development goals. They recognized that building a sustainable supply chain not only mitigates risks but also creates long-term value for their businesses and the broader community.

Community Engagement and Development

Amidst the bustling Zambia Development Forum, a workshop dedicated to community engagement and development drew a diverse group of stakeholders including business leaders, community organizers, and government officials. Chanda Mwamba, a respected community development consultant, took center stage to explore the significance of community engagement and share best practices. Among the attendees were Mutinta Mwiinga, a passionate agribusiness entrepreneur, and Wamundila Chikumbi, a tech innovator committed to fostering positive community relationships.

Importance of Community Engagement

Chanda began, her voice resonating with empathy and determination, "Good morning, esteemed guests. Today, we delve into the critical role of community engagement in sustainable business practices. Engaging with communities not only builds trust and goodwill but also fosters mutual understanding and supports inclusive development."

Thandiwe Zulu, a community relations expert, joined in, "In Zambia, successful businesses recognize that community engagement is integral to their social license to operate. It involves listening to community needs, addressing concerns, and collaborating on initiatives that benefit both businesses and communities."

Best Practices for Community Development

Kalenga Mukuka, a development strategist, continued, "Best practices include conducting thorough needs assessments, establishing transparent communication channels, and implementing community-driven development projects. Collaboration with local stakeholders ensures projects align with community priorities and contribute to sustainable socio-economic development."

Mutinta raised her hand, "Could you provide examples of successful community projects?"

Thandiwe shared enthusiastically, "Certainly! A notable example is a mining company that partnered with local communities to build schools and provide scholarships for students. Another case involves a manufacturing plant that initiated skills training programs, enhancing local employment opportunities and workforce development."

Case Studies of Successful Community Projects

Wamundila, eager to learn from practical examples, asked, "Can you share more case studies of successful community projects in Zambia?"

Chanda nodded, "Absolutely. One inspiring initiative is a renewable energy company that installed solar-powered water pumps in rural communities, improving access to clean water and promoting sustainable agriculture. Another example involves a telecommunications company that established digital literacy programs, empowering youth and promoting digital inclusion."

Conclusion

As the workshop concluded, participants exchanged ideas and committed to enhancing their community engagement strategies. Mutinta and Wamundila left inspired, understanding that meaningful community engagement not only strengthens business operations but also contributes to Zambia's sustainable development goals. They were determined to implement inclusive practices that fostered positive relationships with communities, ensuring mutual benefit and long-term prosperity.

Sustainability Reporting and Transparency

In the grand halls of the Lusaka Sustainability Summit, a seminar on sustainability reporting and transparency gathered a diverse group of business leaders, sustainability professionals, and investors. Chanda Mwamba, a seasoned sustainability consultant, stood at the podium, poised to delve into the intricacies of sustainability reporting. Among the audience were Mutinta Mwiinga, an ambitious agribusiness owner, and Wamundila Chikumbi, a tech entrepreneur with a keen interest in corporate transparency.

Importance of Sustainability Reporting

Chanda began, her voice carrying authority and conviction, "Good afternoon, esteemed guests. Today, we explore the critical importance of sustainability reporting in driving transparency and accountability within businesses. Sustainable practices not only benefit the environment and society but also enhance business resilience and attract responsible investors."

Thandiwe Zulu, a sustainability reporting specialist, added, "In Zambia, sustainability reporting provides stakeholders with insights into a company's environmental, social, and governance (ESG) performance. It demonstrates commitment to ethical business practices, regulatory compliance, and long-term value creation."

Key Reporting Frameworks and Standards

Kalenga Mukuka, a corporate governance expert, continued, "Reporting frameworks such as the Global Reporting Initiative (GRI), Sustainable Development Goals (SDGs), and Carbon Disclosure Project (CDP) guide companies in disclosing ESG metrics. These frameworks ensure consistency, comparability, and credibility in sustainability disclosures."

Mutinta raised her hand, "How can businesses navigate these reporting frameworks effectively?"

Thandiwe explained, "Businesses should align reporting with their strategic goals, engage stakeholders in materiality assessments to identify key ESG issues, and integrate sustainability into corporate governance structures. Regular audits and independent verification enhance credibility and transparency of sustainability reports."

Conclusion

As the seminar concluded, participants exchanged insights and strategies for enhancing sustainability reporting practices in Zambia. Mutinta and Wamundila left inspired, recognizing that transparent reporting not only fosters trust with stakeholders but also drives continuous improvement in sustainability performance. They were determined to implement robust reporting frameworks that align with international standards, demonstrating their commitment to responsible business practices and contributing to Zambia's sustainable development agenda.

9

Chapter 9: Market Research and Due Diligence

Conducting Feasibility Studies and Business Plans

At the Zambia Business Expo, amidst the vibrant atmosphere of innovation and entrepreneurship, a workshop on conducting feasibility studies and crafting business plans attracted a diverse audience of aspiring entrepreneurs, seasoned business owners, and financial experts. Chanda Mwamba, a renowned business strategist, stood before the eager crowd, ready to unravel the intricacies of feasibility studies and business planning. Among the attendees were Mutinta Mwiinga, an enterprising agribusiness owner, and Wamundila Chikumbi, a tech visionary with aspirations to expand his startup.

Importance of Feasibility Studies

Chanda began, her voice resonating with clarity and authority, "Good morning, esteemed entrepreneurs and investors. Today, we delve into the pivotal role of feasibility studies in shaping successful business ventures. A feasibility study provides a structured approach to assessing the viability of a business idea, identifying potential challenges, and defining clear paths to profitability."

Thandiwe Zulu, a financial consultant, added, "In Zambia, conducting a feasibility study ensures informed decision-making and risk management. It evaluates market demand, competitive landscape, operational feasibility, and financial projections, offering valuable insights to entrepreneurs and investors."

Key Components of a Feasibility Study

Kalenga Mukuka, a business analyst, continued, "Key components include market analysis, assessing technical feasibility, conducting financial projections, and evaluating regulatory compliance. A well-executed feasibility study mitigates risks, validates business assumptions, and enhances investor confidence."

Mutinta raised her hand, "What are the essential elements of a comprehensive business plan?"

Thandiwe responded, "A business plan outlines the business concept, market strategy, organizational structure, financial forecasts, and growth projections. It serves as a roadmap for achieving business objectives, securing financing, and guiding day-to-day operations."

Developing a Comprehensive Business Plan

Wamundila, eager to refine his startup strategy, asked, "How can entrepreneurs develop a compelling business plan?"

Chanda smiled, "Start by defining a clear vision and mission statement, conducting thorough market research, and outlining a robust marketing and sales strategy. Incorporate financial projections, operational plans, and risk management strategies. A well-crafted business plan not only attracts investors but also aligns team efforts and ensures strategic alignment."

Conclusion

As the workshop concluded, participants engaged in lively discussions and exchanged contact information for future collaborations. Mutinta and Wamundila left inspired, equipped with practical insights and tools to conduct feasibility studies and develop comprehensive business plans that would pave the way for their entrepreneurial success in Zambia's dynamic market landscape. They were determined to apply their newfound knowledge, confident in their ability to navigate challenges and seize opportunities in their respective industries.

Competitive Analysis and Benchmarking

In the heart of the Zambia Business Summit, a strategy session focused on competitive analysis and benchmarking drew a diverse crowd of business executives, market analysts, and ambitious entrepreneurs. Chanda Mwamba, a seasoned strategist, took the stage with confidence, prepared to dissect the nuances of competitive analysis and share strategies for achieving market dominance. Among the attendees were Mutinta Mwiinga, an innovative agribusiness entrepreneur, and Wamundila Chikumbi, a tech disruptor eager to establish his startup.

Overview of Competitive Analysis

Chanda began, her voice commanding attention, "Good afternoon, esteemed guests. Today, we explore the critical importance of competitive analysis in navigating Zambia's dynamic market landscape. Competitive analysis entails evaluating competitors' strengths, weaknesses, market positioning, and strategies to gain insights and inform strategic decisions."

Thandiwe Zulu, a market intelligence specialist, interjected, "In Zambia, businesses conduct competitive analysis to identify market trends, customer preferences, and emerging threats. It provides a comprehensive view of the competitive environment, enabling businesses to capitalize on opportunities and mitigate risks."

Benchmarking Against Industry Leaders

Kalenga Mukuka, a strategic planner, continued, "Benchmarking involves comparing your business performance and practices against industry leaders and best-in-class companies. It helps identify gaps, set performance targets, and implement industry best practices to achieve operational excellence."

Mutinta raised her hand, "How can businesses effectively gain a competitive advantage?"

Thandiwe responded, "Strategies include differentiation through product innovation, enhancing customer experience, optimizing supply chain efficiency, and leveraging technology for operational excellence. By continuously monitoring market dynamics and adapting strategies, businesses can stay ahead of competitors."

Conclusion

As the session concluded, participants engaged in spirited discussions and shared their perspectives on implementing competitive analysis strategies in their businesses. Mutinta and Wamundila left inspired, equipped with actionable insights and strategies to conduct competitive analysis, benchmark against industry leaders, and leverage their strengths to achieve sustainable growth and success in Zambia's competitive market landscape. They were eager to apply their newfound knowledge, confident in their ability to navigate challenges and capitalize on opportunities to elevate their businesses to new heights.

Risk Assessment and Mitigation

Amidst the Lusaka Business Conference, a focused workshop on risk assessment and mitigation strategies attracted a diverse group of entrepreneurs, risk managers, and financial experts. Chanda Mwamba, a seasoned risk management consultant, stood before the audience, ready to delve into the critical aspects of identifying risks, implementing mitigation strategies, and the importance of contingency planning. Among the participants were Mutinta Mwiinga, an ambitious agribusiness owner, and Wamundila Chikumbi, a tech entrepreneur keen on safeguarding his startup against potential pitfalls.

Identifying Potential Risks

Chanda began, her voice authoritative yet reassuring, "Good morning, esteemed attendees. Today, we address the pivotal role of risk assessment in strategic business planning. Identifying potential risks involves analyzing internal and external factors that could impact business operations, financial stability, and market positioning."

Thandiwe Zulu, a risk management expert, added, "In Zambia's dynamic market environment, common risks include economic volatility, regulatory changes, technological disruptions, and competitive pressures. Conducting a thorough risk assessment enables businesses to proactively anticipate challenges and devise appropriate mitigation strategies."

Risk Mitigation Strategies

Kalenga Mukuka, a strategic advisor, continued, "Effective risk mitigation strategies include diversifying revenue streams, implementing robust financial controls, securing insurance coverage, and building strong supplier and customer relationships. By mitigating identified risks, businesses enhance resilience and safeguard their long-term sustainability."

Mutinta raised her hand, "How important is contingency planning in risk management?"

Thandiwe responded emphatically, "Contingency planning is crucial as it ensures businesses are prepared to respond swiftly and effectively to unforeseen events or crises. It involves developing alternative action plans, maintaining liquidity reserves, and establishing crisis communication protocols to mitigate potential impacts on operations and reputation."

Conclusion

As the workshop concluded, participants engaged in discussions, sharing insights and strategies for enhancing risk management practices in their respective businesses. Mutinta and Wamundila left empowered, equipped with practical knowledge and tools to conduct thorough risk assessments, implement effective mitigation strategies, and develop robust contingency plans. They were determined to integrate these practices into their business strategies, confident in their ability to navigate uncertainties and seize opportunities in Zambia's competitive business landscape.

10

Chapter 10: The Future of Investment in Zambia

Emerging Investment Trends

The Lusaka International Conference Center was abuzz with activity. Delegates from across the globe had gathered for the annual International Investment Summit. The event promised to unveil the future investment landscape of Zambia, with speakers from various sectors ready to share their insights. Among the key speakers were Mr. Kalaba, an economist specializing in African markets; Ms. Tembo, a regional investment strategist; and Mr. Mwansa, a successful entrepreneur.

Overview of Global and Regional Investment Trends

Mr. Kalaba took the stage first, addressing the packed hall. "Ladies and gentlemen, it's a pleasure to be here today to discuss the emerging investment trends that are shaping our world.

Globally, we are witnessing a shift towards sustainable and impact investments. Investors are increasingly looking for opportunities that not only provide financial returns but also contribute positively to society and the environment."

He continued, "Regionally, Africa is gaining traction as a prime investment destination. Factors such as a growing middle class, urbanization, and improvements in infrastructure are driving this interest. Countries like Zambia, with their abundant natural resources and strategic location, are well-positioned to benefit from these trends."

Implications for Zambia

Ms. Tembo then took the microphone, "Thank you, Mr. Kalaba. To build on those points, let's discuss what these global and regional trends mean for Zambia. As investors look for new opportunities, Zambia stands out due to its stable political environment, investment-friendly policies, and ongoing economic reforms."

She highlighted, "One major implication is the potential for increased foreign direct investment (FDI). Zambia's participation in regional trade blocs like the Southern African Development Community (SADC) and the African Continental Free Trade Area (AfCFTA) opens up new markets and makes Zambia an attractive hub for investment."

Mr. Mwansa, joining the discussion, added, "Moreover, the government's commitment to improving infrastructure and reducing bureaucratic hurdles further enhances the investment climate. This proactive approach is crucial in attracting and retaining investors."

Sectors with High Growth Potential

The focus then shifted to specific sectors poised for significant growth. Mr. Kalaba elaborated, "Agriculture remains a cornerstone of Zambia's economy, and there's immense potential in agribusiness. Innovations in farming techniques and increased access to markets can transform this sector. Additionally, the push towards value addition in agriculture can create new investment opportunities in food processing and packaging."

Ms. Tembo chimed in, "Another sector with high growth potential is mining. Zambia is rich in minerals, and with advancements in mining technology and sustainable practices, the sector can see substantial investments. However, it's not just about traditional minerals; the global shift towards green energy is increasing demand for minerals like cobalt and lithium, which are essential for batteries and renewable energy technologies."

Mr. Mwansa spoke next, "The ICT and telecommunications sector is also ripe for investment. With a growing young population and increasing internet penetration, there's a significant opportunity in digital services and tech startups. Government initiatives to improve ICT infrastructure and promote innovation hubs are creating a fertile ground for this sector to thrive."

Conclusion

As the session came to a close, the speakers emphasized the need for a collaborative approach to harness these opportunities. Mr. Kalaba's closing remarks were a call to action, "Zambia's future as an investment destination is bright, but it requires concerted efforts from the government, private sector, and international partners. By aligning our strategies with emerging trends, we can ensure sustainable and inclusive growth for the nation."

The audience, comprising investors, policymakers, and business leaders, left the summit with a renewed sense of optimism and a clear vision of the opportunities that lay ahead. Lombe Kunda, among the attendees, felt inspired by the discussions. He envisioned leveraging the insights gained to expand his agribusiness venture, tapping into the emerging trends and contributing to Zambia's economic transformation.

With a sense of purpose and a wealth of knowledge, Lombe walked out of the conference center, ready to seize the opportunities that the future held for Zambia and its investors.

Long-Term Economic Growth Projections

The large boardroom was filled with key stakeholders in Zambia's economic development. The Minister of Finance, Ms. Mutinta Banda, had called for this important meeting to discuss the nation's long-term economic growth projections. Among the attendees were Mr. Chanda, the head of the Central Statistical Office; Dr. Phiri, an economic advisor; and Ms. Mwila, a representative from the Zambia Development Agency.

Economic Forecasts for Zambia

Ms. Banda began the meeting with a confident tone. "Thank you all for being here today. We have important work ahead as we project Zambia's economic trajectory over the next decade. Mr. Chanda, could you start by presenting the latest economic forecasts?"

Mr. Chanda stood and projected a graph onto the screen. "Based on our current models, Zambia's GDP is expected to grow at an average rate of 5.5% annually over the next ten years. This growth is driven by a combination of factors, including increased investment in infrastructure, a burgeoning young population, and our strategic efforts to diversify the economy beyond mining."

He continued, "Inflation is projected to stabilize around 6%, thanks to prudent monetary policies. The exchange rate is also expected to remain relatively stable, provided we maintain our current fiscal discipline and continue to attract foreign direct investment."

Key Drivers of Long-Term Growth

Dr. Phiri took over, providing deeper insights into the growth drivers. "The first key driver is the agriculture sector. With ongoing investments in irrigation, modern farming techniques, and rural infrastructure, we expect significant increases in agricultural productivity. Furthermore, the development of agro-processing industries will add value to our primary products and create jobs."

"The second driver is the mining sector," Dr. Phiri added. "While traditional copper mining remains crucial, the global shift towards renewable energy sources is increasing demand for minerals like cobalt and lithium. Zambia's rich deposits of these minerals position us well to benefit from this trend."

Ms. Mwila highlighted another crucial area, "Don't forget the ICT sector. The government's investment in digital infrastructure and initiatives to foster tech innovation are paving the way for Zambia to become a regional leader in digital services. This sector will not only drive economic growth but also improve efficiency across all other sectors."

Potential Challenges and Opportunities

Ms. Banda then addressed the potential challenges. "While our projections are optimistic, we must be mindful of the hurdles. One major challenge is the need for continuous investment in education and skill development. As our economy diversifies, we need a workforce that is equipped with the necessary skills."

Mr. Chanda nodded in agreement, "Another challenge is infrastructure. Despite our progress, there are still gaps in our transportation and energy networks that need addressing to fully support economic growth."

Dr. Phiri added, "We must also be cautious of external factors such as fluctuations in global commodity prices and geopolitical tensions, which could impact our exports and investment inflows."

On a more positive note, Ms. Mwila spoke about opportunities, "The rise of green energy presents a significant opportunity for Zambia. By investing in renewable energy projects, we can reduce our dependence on imported fuels, create jobs, and position ourselves as a leader in sustainable development."

Conclusion

Ms. Banda concluded the meeting, "In light of these forecasts, drivers, and challenges, it's clear that we have both significant opportunities and hurdles ahead. Our task is to ensure that we create an environment conducive to sustainable and inclusive growth. By leveraging our strengths and addressing our weaknesses, we can achieve our vision for Zambia's future."

As the meeting adjourned, the attendees left with a clear mandate and a shared vision. Kunda, a young entrepreneur who had been quietly listening, felt inspired by the discussions. He saw opportunities in the challenges discussed and was determined to contribute to Zambia's growth by investing in renewable energy.

Walking out of the Ministry of Finance, Kunda reflected on the optimistic projections and resolved to take action. He knew that with strategic investments and a focus on sustainable practices, Zambia's future was indeed promising.

Conclusion: Unveiling Zambia's Potential

Amidst the grand setting of the Zambia Economic Forum, distinguished leaders, investors, and policymakers gathered for a keynote address on "Unveiling Zambia's Potential." The keynote speaker, Dr. Mwila Ng'andu, an esteemed economist, stood at the podium, capturing the audience's attention with his profound insights and vision for Zambia's economic future.

"In conclusion," Dr. Ng'andu began, his voice resonating with conviction, "Today, we've explored the diverse facets of Zambia's economic landscape, from its burgeoning sectors to robust infrastructure developments and favorable investment climate. As we look ahead, it's crucial to recognize Zambia's immense potential as a hub for investment and economic growth in the region."

He continued, "With strategic initiatives such as Vision 2030 and comprehensive national development plans, Zambia is poised to harness its natural resources, human capital, and strategic geographical location to drive sustainable economic development. The key lies in fostering innovation, promoting inclusive growth, and enhancing competitiveness across sectors."

Dr. Ng'andu paused, emphasizing, "While we acknowledge the challenges ahead, including global economic uncertainties and domestic reforms, they present opportunities for resilience and adaptation. By leveraging our strengths, nurturing partnerships, and embracing technological advancements, Zambia can navigate these challenges and emerge stronger."

He concluded, "In unveiling Zambia's potential, let us commit to collaborative efforts, responsible investments, and sustainable practices that ensure prosperity for all Zambians. Together, we can realize a future where Zambia thrives as a beacon of opportunity and prosperity in Africa and beyond."

As the audience erupted in applause, inspired by Dr. Ng'andu's vision and optimism, attendees exchanged nods of agreement and shared aspirations for a brighter future. They departed the forum with renewed determination to contribute to Zambia's economic transformation, echoing the sentiment that indeed, Zambia's potential is boundless and ready to be unveiled to the world.

About the Author

Goodson Mumba is a multifaceted individual known for his diverse expertise and prolific contributions across various fields. As an infopreneur, Management Consultant, thought leader, and spiritual leader, he has inspired countless individuals through his insightful teachings and impactful writings. Mumba is also an accomplished author, with several notable works to his name, including "Understanding Corporate Worship," "The Years I Spent in a Week," "Management By Harmony," "The CEO's Diary," "Change to Change" and "Creative Thinking for results" His literary works span topics ranging from business management to personal development and spirituality, reflecting his broad range of interests and insights.

With a Master of Business Leadership (MBL) and a Bachelor of Arts in Theology (BTh), Mumba brings a unique blend of business acumen and spiritual wisdom to his work. His educational background is further enriched by a Group Diploma in Management Studies, providing him with a solid foundation in organizational dynamics and leadership principles. Additionally, Mumba holds diplomas in Education Psychology, Leadership and Management Styles, Organizational Behaviour, Financial Accounting, Economic Growth and Development, and Project Management, showcasing his commitment to continuous learning and professional development.

Mumba's expertise extends beyond traditional academic disciplines, encompassing areas such as Neuro-Linguistic Programming (NLP) and Positive Psychology. His diverse skill set is complemented by a range of certifications, including Creative Problem Solving and Decision Making, Life Coaching Fundamentals and Techniques, Professional Life Coaching, and Performance Management System Design. These certifications reflect Mumba's dedication to equipping himself with the tools and knowledge necessary to empower others and drive positive change.

As an author, Mumba's writings reflect his deep understanding of human nature, organizational dynamics, and spiritual principles. His works offer practical insights, actionable strategies, and inspirational guidance for individuals seeking personal growth, professional success, and spiritual fulfillment. Mumba's holistic approach to life and leadership resonates with readers worldwide, making him a respected figure in both the business and spiritual communities.

Overall, Goodson Mumba's diverse background, extensive knowledge, and profound insights make him a sought-after speaker, mentor, and author. His commitment to excellence, lifelong learning, and service to others continues to inspire individuals to unlock their full potential and lead lives of purpose and significance.

Goodson Mumba is renowned for initiating the concept of Management by Harmony, revolutionizing traditional management practices with a focus on balanced and holistic approaches. He has authored two influential books on this subject: "Introduction to Management by Harmony" and its sequel, "Management by Harmony."

Mumba's work has significantly impacted the field, offering innovative strategies for fostering organizational harmony and efficiency. His contributions continue to shape contemporary management theories and practices.